DAUERHAFT
EVERLASTING

CAROLIN WÜBBELS

Florale Dekorationen für gewerbliche und private Räume
Floral decorations for offices and homes

Sponsored by

NEWBARCELO
NALIGHTCOPE
NHANGENFRES
HAMSTERDAM
YOUNGBRITISH
COSYBRUXELL
ESNEWBARCEL
ONALIGHTCOPE
NHANGENFRES

Herausgeber · Publisher
BLOOM's GmbH, Ratingen (D)
www.blooms.de

Konzeption & Idee · Concept & Idea
Marion Bauer

Floralkonzept & Styling · Floral Concept & Styling
Carolin Wübbels

Floraldesign · Floral Design
Petra Böttger, Steffi Dix, Olga Rehm, Carolin Wübbels

Redaktion & Text · Editorial & Text
Hella Henckel

Fotos · Photography
Patrick Pantze-Werbefotografie GmbH, Lage (D)

Grafikdesign · Graphic Design
Carolin Hetzel

DTP · DTP
Gordian Jenal

Übersetzung · Translation
Kern AG, Bonn (D)

Herstellung · Production
Egedsa, Sabadell (E)

IMPRESSUM
IMPRINT

© BLOOM's GmbH
Am Potekamp 6
D-40885 Ratingen
T +49 2102 9644-0
F +49 2102 896073
www.blooms.de
info@blooms.de

1. Auflage 2012

ISBN 978-3-939868-72-9

Das Werk ist urheberrechtlich geschützt. Jede Verwertung ist ohne schriftliche Zustimmung des Verlages oder des Herausgebers unzulässig. Dies gilt insbesondere für Vervielfältigungen, Übersetzungen, Mikroverfilmungen sowie deren Einspeicherung und Verarbeitung in elektronischen Systemen.
This book is protected by copyright. No reproduction in any form is permissible without the express, prior written approval of the publishers or editors. This applies in particular to copying, translations, microfilming and storage or processing by electronic systems.

INHALT CONTENTS

008

042

058

NEWBARCELONA   FRESHAMSTERDAM   YOUNGBRITISH

LIGHTCOPENHAGEN

COSYBRUXELLES

Impressum 003
Imprint

Inhalt 004
Contents

Vorwort 006
Foreword

Service 126
Service

VORWORT
FOREWORD

Räumen Seele geben

Räume ohne Grün oder florale Komponente wirken uninspiriert, kühl und unpersönlich. Doch nicht immer lässt sich frisches Grün in Form lebender Pflanzen und Blumen einbringen. Standortbedingungen wie wenig Helligkeit, trockene Raumluft, keine oder wenig Pflegemöglichkeiten lassen den Einsatz künstlicher oder trockener Produkte als sinnvoll erscheinen. Und diese stehen ihren natürlichen Vorbildern in nichts nach! Eine hohe Qualität der Materialien, eine naturgetreue Nachbildung mit detailreicher Ausgestaltung, farblich perfekter Imitation und eine Kombination mit getrockneten Naturmaterialien machen Floralgestaltungen dieser Art zu einer optimalen Alternative.

Dauerhafte Floralgestaltungen hauchen öffentlich zugänglichen Räumen in Hotels, Restaurants, aber auch Wartezonen von Praxen oder privaten Bereichen Seele ein. Wir haben eine Fülle an Gestaltungsideen zusammengestellt, die nahezu alle stilistischen Gegebenheiten abdeckt, von groß bis klein, von verspielt bis reduziert-kühl. Wir hoffen, damit sowohl dem gestaltenden Floristen und Floraldesigner, als auch dem Rezipienten, dem Gastronomen, Hotelbesitzer oder Inhaber von Kanzleien, Praxen oder sonstigen Räumen, in denen sich Menschen aufhalten, Vorschläge an die Hand gegeben zu haben, wie sich Räume freundlich, individualisiert und zum Wohlfühlen gestalten lassen.

Wir wünschen Ihnen viel Erfolg damit!

Carolin Wübbels
und das BLOOM's-Designer- und -Floristenteam

Bringing Rooms to Life

Rooms without houseplant or floral elements feel uninspired, cold and impersonal. However, it is not always practical to introduce something fresh and green in the form of living plants and flowers. Adverse room conditions, such as very little light, dry room air, and little or no scope for plant care make the use of artificial or dried products seem a sensible choice. And they are in no way inferior to the real thing! High-quality materials, authentic replication down to the tiniest detail, colours which exactly imitate life and the chance to combine them with dried natural materials make these kind of flower arrangements the perfect alternative. Permanent floral decorations bring life to public rooms in hotels and restaurants, but also to practice waiting rooms or private spaces. We have compiled a host of design ideas, from unobtrusively small to large-scale, from playful to minimalist and sophisticated, to cover almost the whole range of possible styles. We hope that we have managed to provide some practical ideas for both florists and floral decoration designers, and for the recipients – the caterers and hotel owners, but also those responsible for ensuring that offices, practices or other rooms where a great number of people have to spend longer periods of time are comfortable and friendly, yet also have their own individual style.

We wish you every success in achieving this!

Carolin Wübbels
and the BLOOM's team of designers and florists

NEW HOTEL & GASTRONOMIE
BARCELONA

Weltgewandt und reduziert gestylt präsentieren sich Hotels mit internationalem Charakter, First-Class-Restaurants sowie Räume, wo die Welt zuhause ist: Ein modern-schlichter Stil, der sich über Zurückhaltung und Klarheit beim Design, in der objekthaften Form und reduzierten Farbe definiert. So auch die Floristik. Sie integriert sich schlicht aber natürlich, kompakt, aber immer überraschend.

Hotels with an international character, first-class restaurants and rooms where guests are made to feel at home prefer an urbane and minimalist styling. A modern, plain design style defined by understatement and clear lines, object-based shapes and muted colours. This also applies to the floral decorations, which blend in unobtrusively, naturally, they are compact, yet nevertheless full of surprises.

NEW BARCELONA Lobby | Lobby

LOBBY LOBBY

In Reih und Glied säumen schulterhohe Gefäßarrangements die Wege im Lobby-Bereich – ein freundliches Welcome in hellen Farben und mit edlen Blüten. Fallopia wird dazu in Steckschaum gesteckt. Aufgeklebte Holzfurnierrechtecke bilden interessante Akzente.

Like sentinels, arrangements in shoulder-high vases stand guard along the walkways in the lobby area – a cheerful welcome in light colours with elegant flowers. To achieve this effect, fallopia is attached to floral foam. Interesting accents are provided by glued on, oblong pieces of wood veneer.

NEW BARCELONA Lobby | Lobby

TIPP! TIP!

Das Kabel der Lampe farblich passend umkleben. In dem handelsfertigen Weidenzweige-Gestell Zweige waagerecht einfügen, in der Mitte kreuzförmig fixieren und hierauf die Lampe platzieren.

Cover the lamp's cable in a matching colour. Thread twigs horizontally through the willow rod base structure, which can be bought ready-made. Secure them where they cross in the centre, then attach the lamp on the resultant platform.

012 | 013

Lampen ruhen auf einem hohen Holzgerüst, das von langen Zweigen kaschiert wird. Somit wird der Blütenschmuck im Überkopfbereich von innen heraus beleuchtet. Farblich und materialmäßig passen dazu vier kleine Gefäßsäulen mit Holzscheiben-Kragen.

Lights are supported by tall wooden base structures concealed with long canes. From these, the floral decorations which have been attached at above head height are lighted up from within. Matching these both in terms of colours and materials used are the four small pillar vases with log slice collar.

NEW BARCELONA Lounge | Lounge

LOUNGE LOUNGE

Three half-spheres, covered in different materials with the aid of adhesive, accentuate the orchid. One of the half-spheres features green-lacquered pieces of wood veneer, applied in a random pattern, another brown wood veneer or cork. Slightly tilted and attached to a metal stand with a spike, the arrangement allows the aerial root of the plant remains visible.

Drei Halbkugeln, die unterschiedlich beklebt werden, verleihen der Orchidee den besonderen Auftritt. Einmal ist die Halbkugel kreuz und quer mit grün lasiertem Furnierstücken versehen, ein anderes Mal mit braunem Holzfurnier oder Kork beklebt. Schräg auf einen Metallständer gesteckt, bietet dies Einblicke auf die Pflanze.

NEW BARCELONA Lounge | Lounge

An einem Steckschaumzylinder auf Metallständer ist der Fadenvorhang befestigt, der zirka auf halber Höhe einen floralen Schmuck in Form aufgeklebter Blüten und Zweige trägt. Die Miniausführung für den Tisch trägt einen Hortensien-Blütenstand on top.

A string curtain has been attached to a floral foam cylinder on a metal stand. Floral decorations in the form of flowers and twigs are glued onto the floral foam, at around the middle of the arrangement's total height. The top of the mini table-top version displays a hydrangea head.

TIPP! TIP!

Der Stiel der kleinen Fadenvorhänge wird veredelt, indem einzelne Fäden herumgewickelt werden. Zum besseren Halt wird der Stiel zuvor mit doppelseitigem Klebeband präpariert.

The small string curtains are made more elegant by wrapping single strands around the stem. To make them more sturdy, the stem is prepared with double-sided adhesive tape.

NEW BARCELONA Empfang | Reception

EMPFANG RECEPTION

Moderne Gefäße mit gerundetem Boden sind mit aufgerolltem Furnier oder Netzband, sowie mit Schoten gefüllt. Kubisch geht's bei dem Würfelensemble zu. Die Trockenfloralien und Orchideen fußen in Steckschaum.

Modern containers with rounded bottoms are filled with curled veneer or net ribbon and pods. The arrangement in the square containers is decidedly cubism-inspired. The dried floral elements and orchids are kept steady by floral foam.

NEW BARCELONA Restaurant | Restaurant

Wirkungsvoll und doch eine schnelle und einfach herzustellende Sache! Das Gestell, mit Splittstäben verankert, steht in dem Sandbett des Gefäßes und wird lediglich mit den Floralien sowie der Orchideenpflanze getoppt. Im Restaurant lassen sich mit solch einem Gefäß-Duo wunderbar privatere Bereiche abtrennen, ohne gänzlich abtrennende Wirkung. Als besonderer Clou sind die Schnittflächen der Zweige mit Farbe akzentuiert.

RESTAURANT RESTAURANT

Impressive yet easy and quick to make! The base structure, anchored with split bamboo canes, stands in a bed of sand at the bottom of the container. The floral elements and the orchid plant merely rest on the top. This type of container-duo is perfect used as a screen to afford some privacy in the restaurant without the use of a solid partition. A clever touch: the cut edges of the twigs are accentuated by painting them.

NEW BARCELONA Restaurant | Restaurant

Mehrere mit Tapete beklebte Steckschaumzylinder sind auf ein geweißtes Brett geklebt und mit Floralien besteckt. In der Menge wirkt dies klar und konzentriert – passend zum Interieur-Stil. Ergänzend dazu die Tischvariante, ebenfalls mit einer Tapeten-Akzentuierung.

Several floral foam cylinders have been covered in wallpaper and attached to a whitened board, then decorated with floral elements attached with adhesive. Taken as a whole, the arrangement looks uncluttered and focused to match the style of the interior. To complement these, a tabletop version, the textured accent again provided by wallpaper.

NEW BARCELONA Restaurant | Restaurant

Strukturtapete gibt übereinander fixierten Steckschaumquadern die besondere Oberfläche. Das Trio auf Stab mit Steinfuß eint der im oberen Drittel umlegte Floralschmuck aus Ranken und Blüten. Er wird von eingesteckten Reedstäben gehalten. Ein Gräserbündel stellt bei dem Tischgefäß die Gefäßverlängerung dar, aus der sich die Orchidee in die Höhe reckt.

Embossed wallpaper adds a special texture to these layers of floral foam bricks. The trio on metal rods inserted in a stone base is decoratively united at the top third of their height by floral elements comprising vines and flowers. It is supported by integral giunco sticks. A bushel of grasses extends the table-top arrangement's container visually, surrounding a tall orchid.

NEW BARCELONA Restaurant | Restaurant

Oft wird nur eine kleine Tischdekoration aufgrund von Platzmangel gewünscht. Da bieten sich kleine Gefäße mit einem Schmuck in einfacher Herstellungstechnik an. Hier sind es Grün-, Senf- bis Brauntöne, die auch durch die künstlichen Floralien aufgegriffen werden. Holzfurnier oder Korb oder beim Flaschentrio das mit Steinen beklebte Teichfolienband und die lediglich eingestellten Floralien sind die Hingucker.

Frequently, only small table-top decorations are required to save space. Small containers with arrangements which are easy to make are the perfect choice. Here, shades of green, mustard and brown have been used, and are also reflected by the artificial flowers. Wood veneer or coir or, in the case of the bottle trio, pebble edging pond liner, and the floral elements, simply held by the containers, are the eye-catching feature.

NEW BARCELONA Restaurant | Restaurant

Konsequent die einmal gewählten Farben aufzugreifen, ist das Geheimnis gelungenen Stylings. In der Farbe der Gefäße sowie der der Floralien zieht sich Grün, Braun und Kiwi wie ein roter Faden durch. Ein Gitter aus Bambusrohrringen akzentuiert die senkrecht eingesteckten Floralien beim Gefäßtrio. Die Flaschen in den Kuben sind geheimnisvoll von Fäden umsponnen, was den Orchideen Halt gibt.

The secret of successful styling is picking up the chosen colours time and again. The colour of the containers as well as the floral elements used all feature green, brown and kiwi-green. A trellis made from bamboo cane rings accentuates the vertically inserted floral elements in the container trio. The cubes used to display the bottles have been covered in string to add a touch of the mystic, as well as to steady the orchids.

NEW BARCELONA Bar | Bar

030 | 031

Stilprägend ist die besondere Holzform, die gespickt wird mit Reedstäben und rundlichen Floralien. Raues Holz mit edel wirkenden Floralien in zurückhaltenden Farben ist eine Kombination, die den Charakter moderner, repräsentativer Räume unterstreicht und stark den Zeitgeist widerspiegelt.

BAR BAR

The character of these arrangement is defined by the unusual wooden shapes, intermixed with giunco sticks and round floral elements. The combination of rough wood and elegant-looking floral elements emphasises the contemporary character of modern prestigious rooms as it strongly reflects the Zeitgeist.

NEW BARCELONA Bar | Bar

Ob im Großen oder Kleinen, auf Füße gestellt, wirken hier die rauen Holzskulpturen leichter und wohnlicher. Sie werden angebohrt und mit den künstlichen Floralien besteckt. Das geht schnell und ist eine wirtschaftlich interessante Idee für gewerbliche Räume.

Whether tall or small with feet, these rough wooden sculptures lighten up the atmosphere, making it homelike. Holes are drilled into them to hold the artificial floral elements. Easy and quick to make, an economical and interesting idea for all commercial premises.

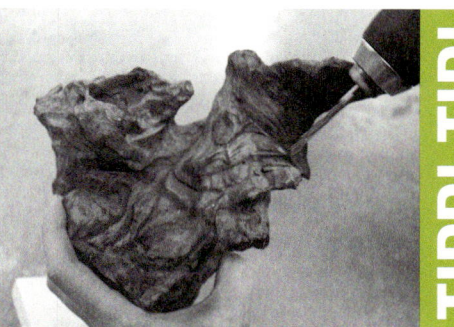

TIPP! TIP!

Zur Fixierung der Wurzel wird diese angebohrt und auf den Ständer mit Metallspieß gesteckt. Auch die Floralien werden in gebohrte Löcher gesteckt.

To give the root a firm footing, drill a hole into it, then place on a stand with a metal spike attached. The floral elements are also inserted into pre-drilled holes.

NEW BARCELONA Bar | Bar

Ein bandartiger Floralschmuck ziert sowohl die Skulptur, bei der ein Drahtgitter das u-förmige Schmuckstück – auf zwei Bambusstangen mit Betonsockel sitzend – bildet, als auch den Paravent aus Bambusstangen.

Ribbon-like floral decorations adorn the sculpture – created by a U-shaped piece of wire mesh attached to two bamboo canes on a concrete base – as well as the bamboo cane screen.

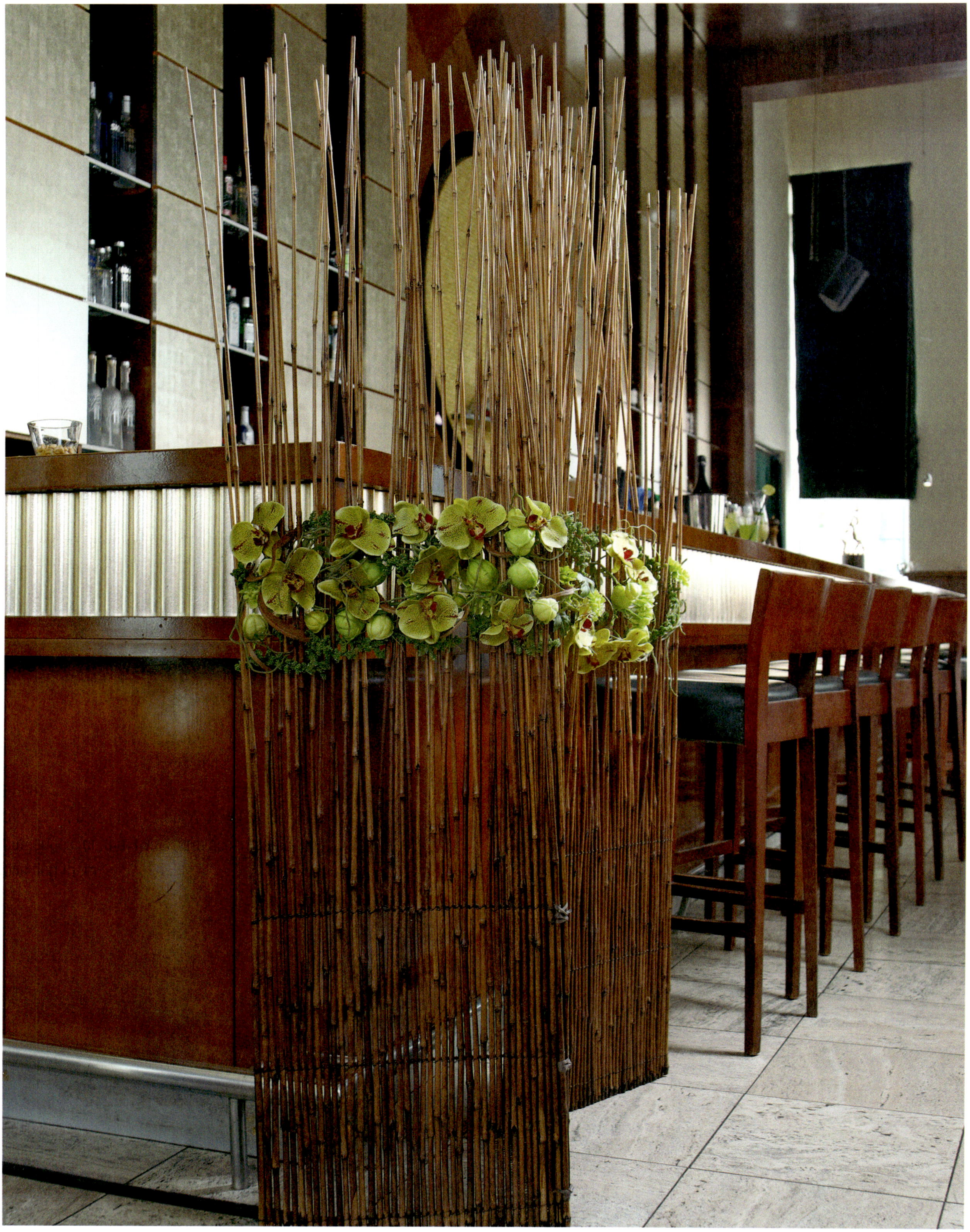

NEW BARCELONA Hotelzimmer | Room

Perfekt unperfekt ist die Devise, wenn Lässigkeit selbstverständlich ist und dennoch schnell und gekonnt inszeniert sein will. Ein verholzter Palmfruchtstand bildet die Basis dieser Säule, er ist an einem Holzstab fixiert, der den Eisenständer verlängert. Die blühenden, künstlichen Floralien werden aufgeklebt, wobei sie im oben Bereich verdichtet, über den Fruchtstand nach unten sich vereinzelnd angebracht werden.

HOTELZIMMER ROOM

Perfect imperfection is the motto when casualness is a given yet must also be contrived, skilfully and quickly. A lignified palm fruit seed head is the basis of this pillar; it has been attached to a wooden pole which extends the metal stand. Artificial flowers in bloom are attached with adhesive, densely packed in the upper part, then gradually less densely towards the bottom of the seed head.

NEW BARCELONA — Hotelzimmer | Room

Arrangements near beds should be space-saving, tall and narrow to avoid them being in the guests' way. Various floral elements in similar colours have been arranged in small and high vases with a broken-looking rim, the arrangement on the bedside table thus matches the arrangement on the desk.

Arrangements in Bettnähe sollten schmal sein, damit sie den Gast nicht stören und genügend Platz für andere Ablagen belassen. Schlanke, hohe Gefäße mit einem Rand, der wie gebrochen aussieht, sind parallel mit unterschiedlichen Floralien, jedoch in ähnlicher Farbgebung, besteckt. So passt der Nachttisch- zum Schreibtischschmuck.

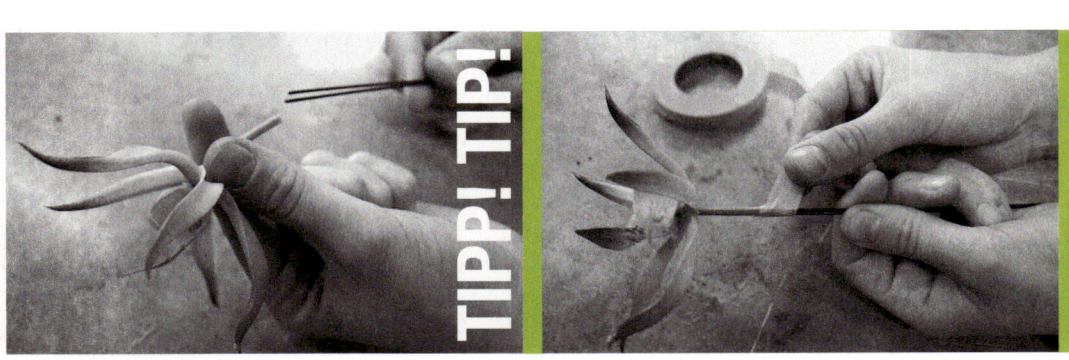

TIPP! TIP!

Einzelne künstliche Orchideenblüten auf zwei Steckdrähte stecken und mit grünem Klebeband umwickeln. So lassen sie sich an längere Stäbe binden oder direkt in die Bündelungen stecken.

Attach single artificial orchids to fixing wire, then cover wire with green adhesive tape. They are now ready to be attached to longer rods or to be inserted directly into bundles.

nachsehen
explore

NEW BARCELONA Hotelzimmer | Room

A nice touch if the theme of the room's floral decorations is picked up in the bathroom, space-saving yet impressive looking, in part doubly-impressive through their reflection in the mirrors. The bushel of grasses looks refreshing, it has been decorated with wood veneer, net ribbon and a strip of pond liner at the foot. The wall arrangement is a board with pods which have been glued onto it in a zigzag pattern. Woody and rough looking pods are complemented by light green seed heads, floral shapes and a vine.

Schön, wenn sich im Bad der florale Raumschmuck fortsetzt, wenig Platz einnehmend und doch mit großer, zum Teil gedoppelter Wirkung durch Spiegelungen. Das Grasbündel erfrischt optisch, sein Fuß ist mit Holzfurnier, Netzband und Teichfolie geschmückt. Die Wanddekoration besteht aus einer im Zickzack mit Schoten beklebten Platte, auf der sich neben den hölzernen, rau wirkenden Schoten hellgrüne Frucht- und Blütenformen sowie eine Ranke finden.

TIPP! TIP!

Die handelsüblichen, künstlichen Grastöpfe werden zur individuellen Anpassung mit schmalen Holzfurnier-Bändern umlegen und beklebt.

Standard artificial grass pots are covered in narrow strips of wood veneer with the aid of adhesive to customise them.

FRESH PRAXIS & AGENTUR
AMSTERDAM

Unkompliziert und im Stil einer frisch-fröhlichen Modernität, das ist eine Ausstrahlung, mit der sich zahlreiche Arztpraxen, Beratungsbüros oder öffentliche Räume schmücken. Wo viele Menschen kurzzeitig verweilen, soll es warmherzig-sympathisch aber auch zeitgemäß-ansprechend zugehen. Zu modernem Mobiliar und frischer Farbgebung setzt der florale Raumschmuck farbliche Akzente.

Uncomplicated, with a touch of fresh and cheery modernism: a style preferred by many a doctor's practice, consulting agency or local government office. Places where a great number of people spend some time waiting, even if only briefly, the atmosphere should be welcoming and warm, yet also contemporary and attractive. Modern furnishings and fresh colourways are accentuated by floral decorations that are eye-catching both in terms of colour and appeal.

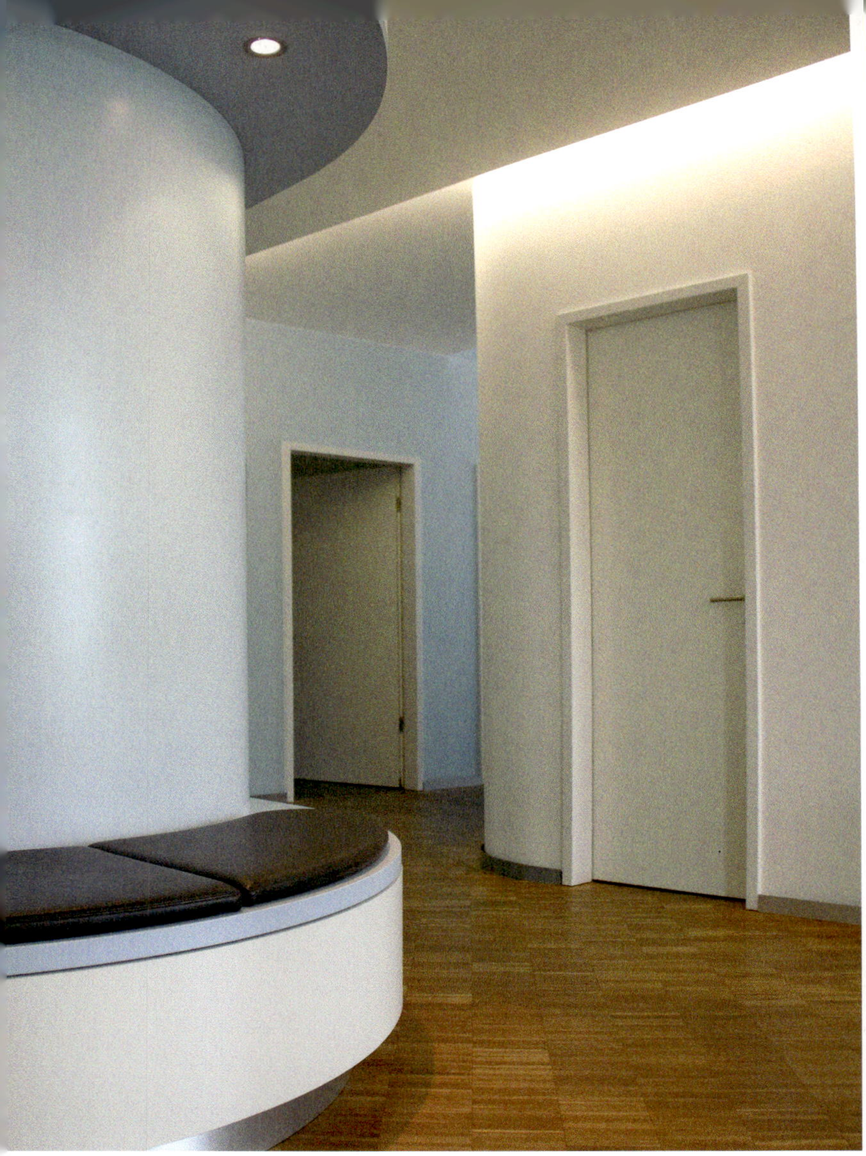
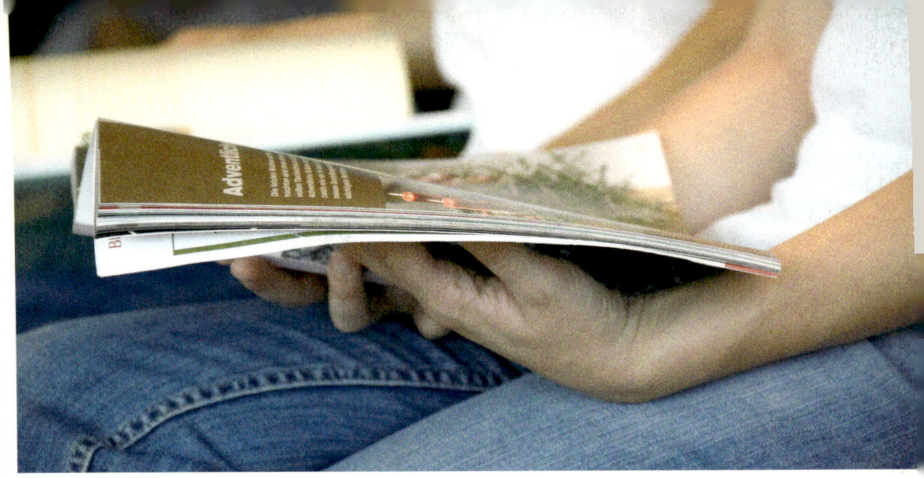
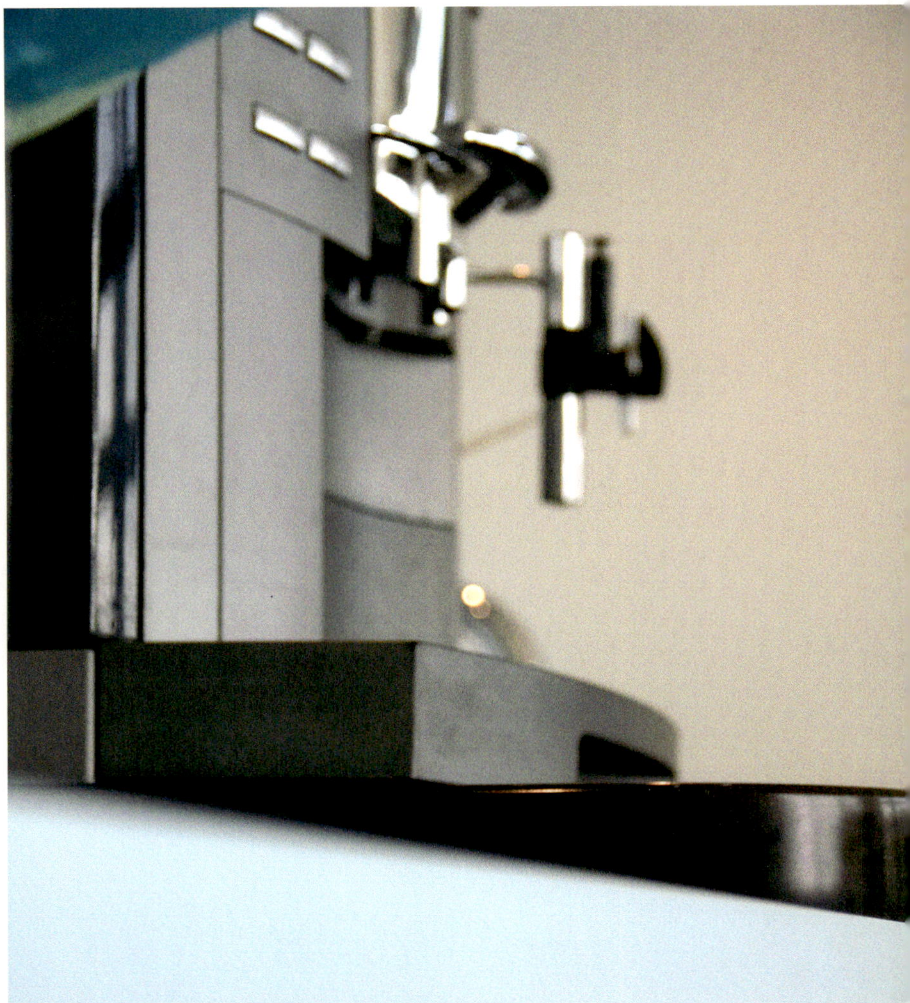
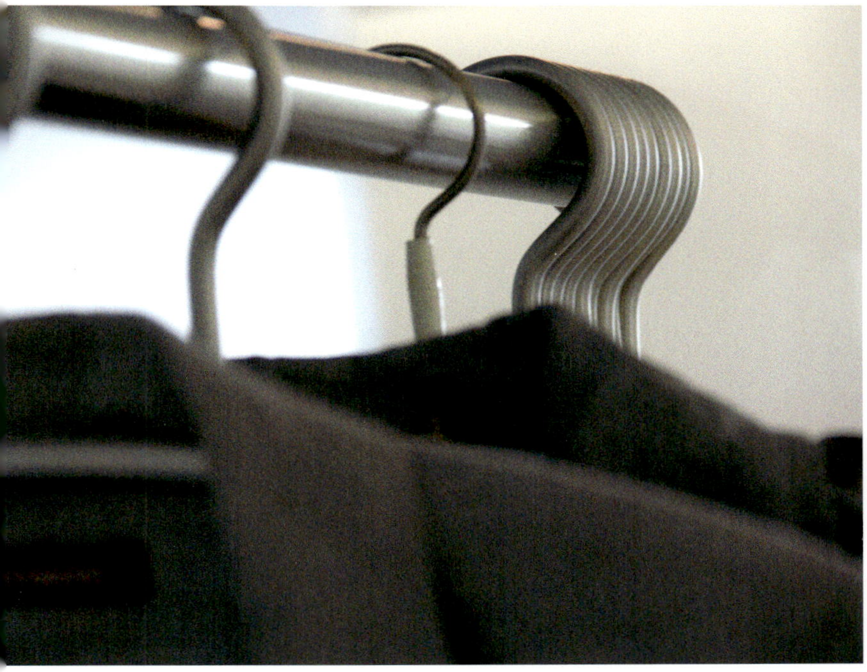
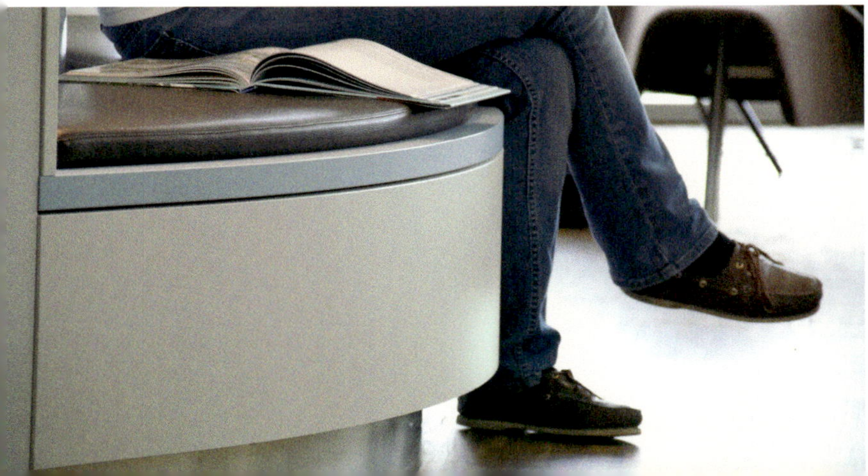
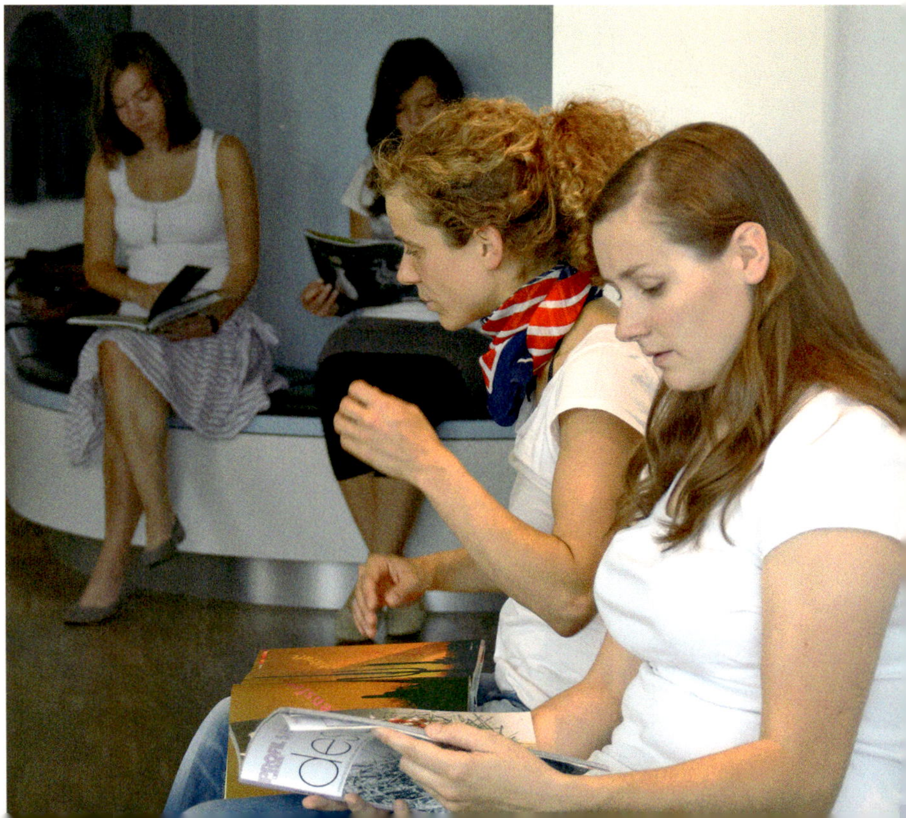

FRESH AMSTERDAM Anmeldung | Reception

ANMELDUNG RECEPTION

Das ist ein wahrer Hingucker! Gefärbtes Seidenpapier (Herstellung siehe Seite 057), das durch Tauchen in Wachs eine gewisse Steifigkeit erhält, wird attraktiv in das Gefäßduo gesteckt. Vor diesem türkisfarbenen Hintergrund leuchten die künstlichen Stiefmütterchen in Gelb besonders gut. Blüten mit Charme und Liebreiz, die Beschaulichkeit und Unkompliziertheit ausstrahlen, sind hier ideal. Dazu passt dann auch die trockene und gefärbte Wilde Möhre, die den dunklen Akzent bildet.

A true eye-catcher! Silk paper, dyed blue (for instructions, see page 057) and made slightly rigid through waxing, is attractively arranged in two matching vases. The yellow, artificial pansies look particularly striking against this turquoise background. Charming, lovely flowers, radiating serenity and artlessness, are perfect for an arrangement like this. In keeping with this, a dark accent is provided by a plain, dried and dyed carrot flower head.

FRESH AMSTERDAM Anmeldung | Reception

TIPP!

Die schönen Farbspuren erhalten die Rollen, wenn man sie kopfüber in die Farbe taucht. Nach der Trocknung Röhren mit Steckschaum und Blumen füllen.

The pretty paint runs are achieved by dipping the paper tubes upside down into paint. Once dry, fill the tubes with floral foam and flowers.

The loveliness of the flowers, as well as their cheerful colours and uncomplicated arrangement, make these decorative concepts suitable floral decorations for a reception area. Forget-me-nots and pansies are inserted into paper tubes with a core of floral foam, they are attached to the bottom of the glasses with pin holders. Below, the flowers are nestling in a bed of moss which has been attached to a floral form base. In the upright bouquet, they are tied together with thick strips of twisted felt to form a compact arrangement which can stand unsupported.

Liebliche Blumen zum einen, fröhliche Farben sowie unkomplizierte Auftritte zum anderen machen diese Dekorationsideen zu passendem Floralschmuck für Wartezonen. Vergissmeinnicht und Stiefmütterchen stecken in Papierröhren, die innen eine Steckschaumseele aufweisen und durch Pinholder am Gefäßboden fixiert werden. Unten ducken sich die Blüten zwischen Moospolster, die auf Steckschaumbasis gehaftet sind. Im Stehstrauß werden sie mit dicken Filzsträngen zu einem handlichen und standfesten Werkstück gebunden.

FRESH AMSTERDAM Anmeldung | Reception

Vasenensembles setzen Farbakzente passend zum CI des Entreebereichs. Steckschaum sorgt für festen und sicheren Halt. Trockenes wird gewachst, zum Teil auch gelackt. Rechts sind die Stiefmütterchen zwischen senkrechte Wachsscheiben geklemmt.

Sets of matching vases pick up on the entrance area's corporate image colours. Floral foam provides a solid and safe base. Dried elements are waxed, or sometimes lacquered. The pansies on the right have been wedged between vertical wax discs.

TIPP! TIP!

Spannung bringen Farbakzente, indem zwischen den Craspedien, die in dickflüssige hellblaue Farbe getaucht wurden, auch einige wenige Blüten mit ihrer natürlichen gelben Farbe leuchten.

Colourful accents add excitement, achieved in this case by inserting just a few Craspedias glowing brightly in their natural yellow between Craspedias dipped into thick light-blue paint.

FRESH AMSTERDAM Wartezone | Waiting Area

In größeren Raumbereichen mit viel Platz bietet es sich an, auch Raumobjekte zu platzieren. Vor allem solche schmalen Säulen sind ideal: modern in ihrer Ausstrahlung, raffiniert in der Ausführung. Der in einem Plastikeimer aus Blitzbeton hergestellte Fuß fixiert die Eisenstange. Hier wird Steckschaum aufgesteckt, dann mit Blättern und Filzsträngen umknotet. Die Enden sind für die waagerechte Ausrichtung mit Wachs angestrichen.

WARTEZONE WAITING AREA

Large-scale decorative objects may also be included in arrangements for generously sized areas with plenty of open spaces. Particularly narrow pillars such as these are ideal: they are utterly contemporary, and cleverly worked. The base, made by pouring fast-set concrete into a plastic bucket, holds an iron pole. Floral foam is skewered onto the pole, then covered in leaves and strips of twisted felt, fastened by knotting. Wax is rubbed into the ends to make them stay horizontal.

FRESH AMSTERDAM Wartezone | Waiting Area

Floral decorations must not impede walkways. Narrow wall-hangings are ideal, here picking up a theme humorously provided by the coat rack. A narrow piece of chipboard is painted, then woven objects and artificial flowers are attached to it.

Floraler Schmuck darf Verkehrswege nicht behindern. Schmale Wandbilder sind ideal, hier mit Witz und Bezug auf die Garderobe. Dazu wird eine schmale Spanplatte gestrichen und mit den taschenähnlichen Webobjekten und künstlichen Blüten versehen.

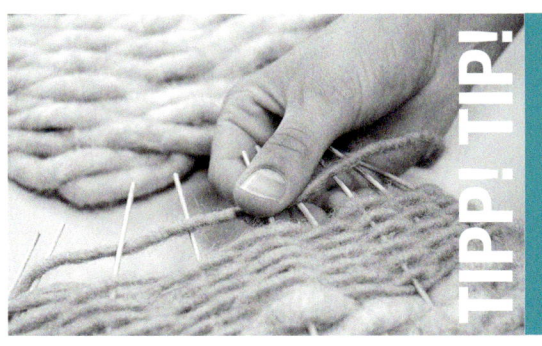

TIPP! TIP!

Für die fächerartigen Webflächen Drähte in vorgebohrte Löcher der Spanplatte stecken, unten weiter auseinander, oben dichter – oder umgekehrt – und mit dicken Filzsträngen durchweben.

To make the fan-like woven elements, wires are inserted into predrilled holes in the chipboard, compact at the bottom and further apart higher up – or the other way round – thick strips of twisted felt are then woven through the wires.

FRESH AMSTERDAM Wartezone | Waiting Area

Styroporplatten sind ideal, um farblich angepasst und mit kreisförmig angeordneten bunten Stäben versehen zu werden. Zwischen diese werden die bunten Blüten gesteckt, so dass die Kranzform deutlich erhalten bleibt.

Styrofoam boards are perfect for colour-matching and decorating with painted sticks, arranged in a circle. Bright flowers are inserted between these to retain the distinct wreath shape.

TIPP! TIP!

Werden einzelne Blüten vorher in weißes Wachs getaucht, werden die Blüten stabiler und bekommen eine glatte Oberfläche.

Dipping single flowers into white wax makes them more durable and gives them a soft surface.

FRESH AMSTERDAM Wartezone | Waiting Area

Wo sich viele Menschen aufhalten, muss floraler Schmuck unempfindlich sein, was die Werkstoffe selbst, ihre Fixierung aber auch die Materialien betrifft. Sand fixiert senkrecht eingestellten Mohn in den Glaskuben, gewachstes Seidenpapier umschützt die Vergissmeinnichtblüten.

Where many people spend time, floral decorations must be durable in terms of the materials themselves, their attachment and the elements used. A sand base ensures that the poppies stay upright in the glass cubes, waxed silkpaper protects the forget-me-nots.

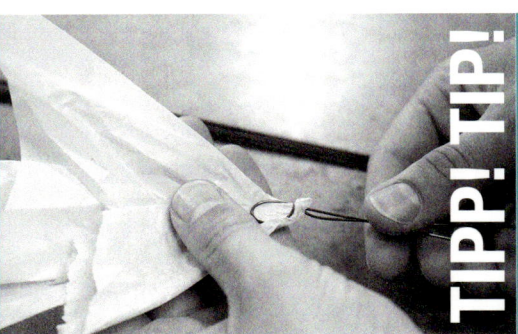

TIPP! TIP!

Kleine Stücke von Seidenpapier andrahten und in farbloses Wachs tauchen. Dann mit den Floralien zum Strauß binden.

Attach wire to small pieces of silk paper and dip into transparent wax, then add them to floral bouquets.

YOUNG BRITISH
SALON & SPA

Ein Hauch Vergangenheit, eine Prise Eleganz und verhaltener Glanz – diese Melange einer mondänen Welt mit Salon und Müßiggang bestimmt die Atmosphäre von Hotels, Varietétheatern oder Opern. Wo man eine kurze Weile der Zeit entrückt genießen möchte, unterstreichen florale Prächtigkeit und blumige Besonderheiten das wieder gesuchte Raumerlebnis vergangener Tage.

A hint of past, a soupcon of elegance, and understated glamour – this melange, reminiscent of a genteel world with drawing rooms and plenty of languorous leisure colours the atmosphere of hotels and venues such as variety theatres of opera houses. In rooms which invite to linger and while away the time, to relax and enjoy, floral resplendence and flowers emphasise the experience of revisiting past pleasurable moments.

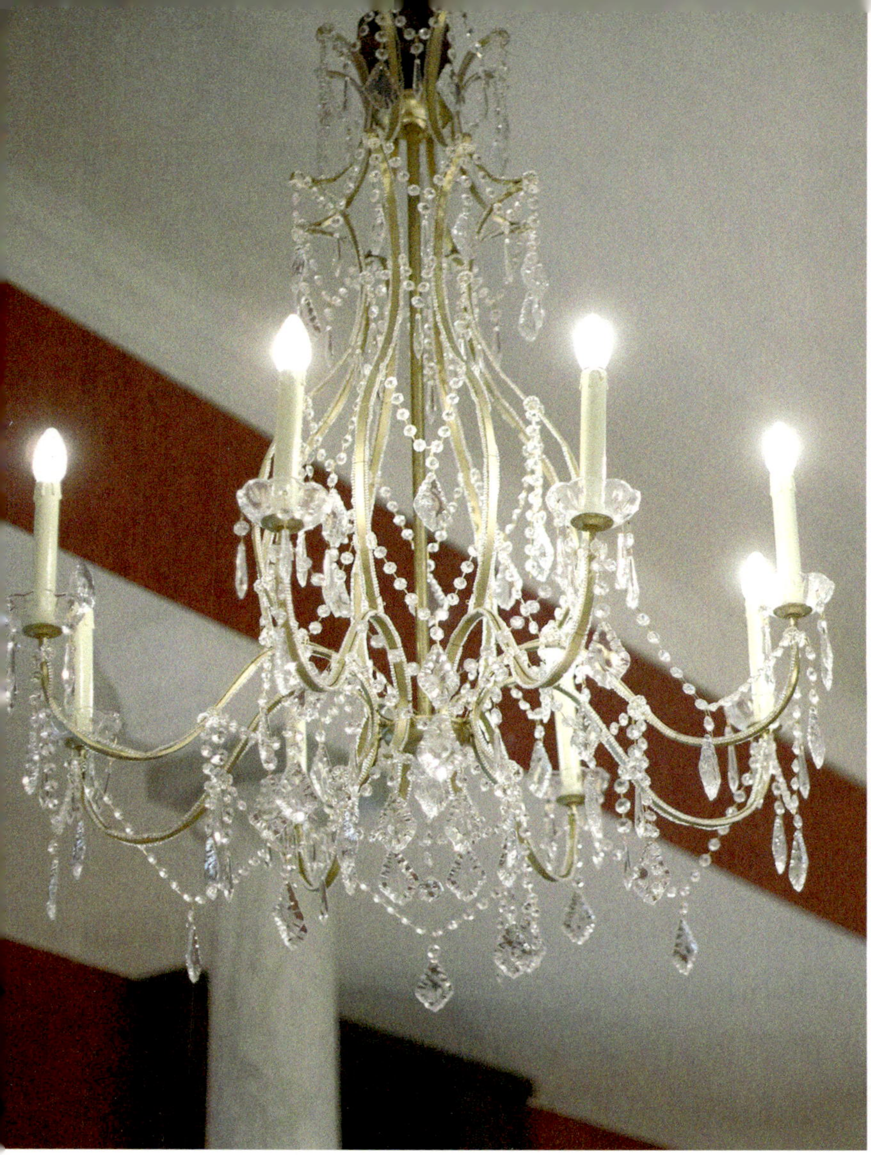
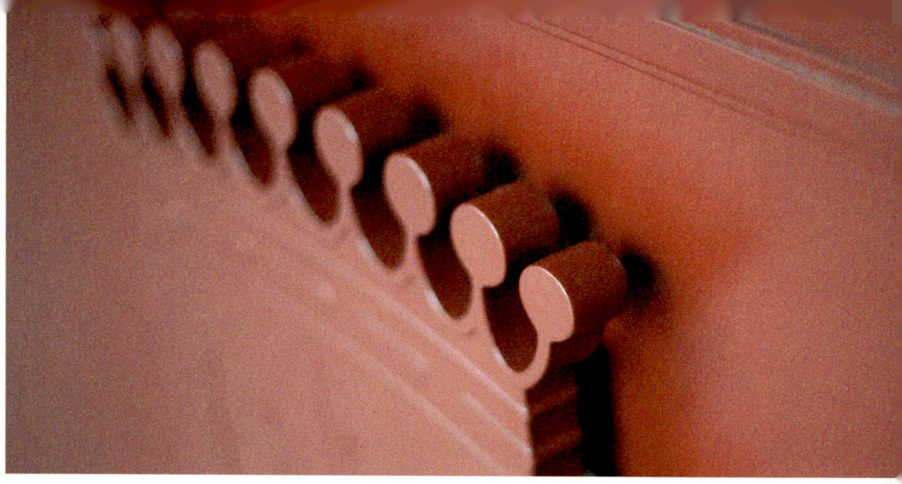
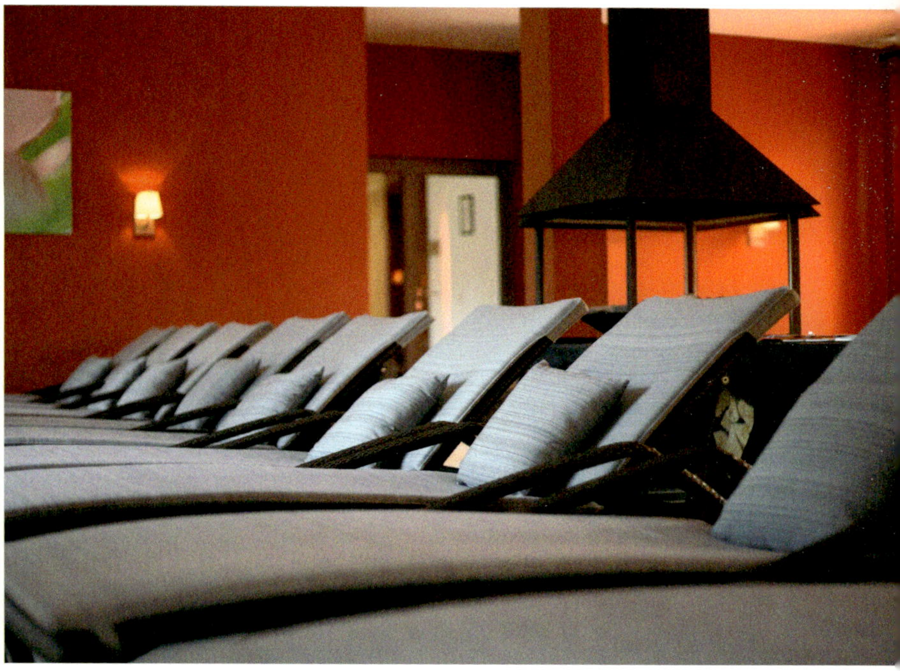
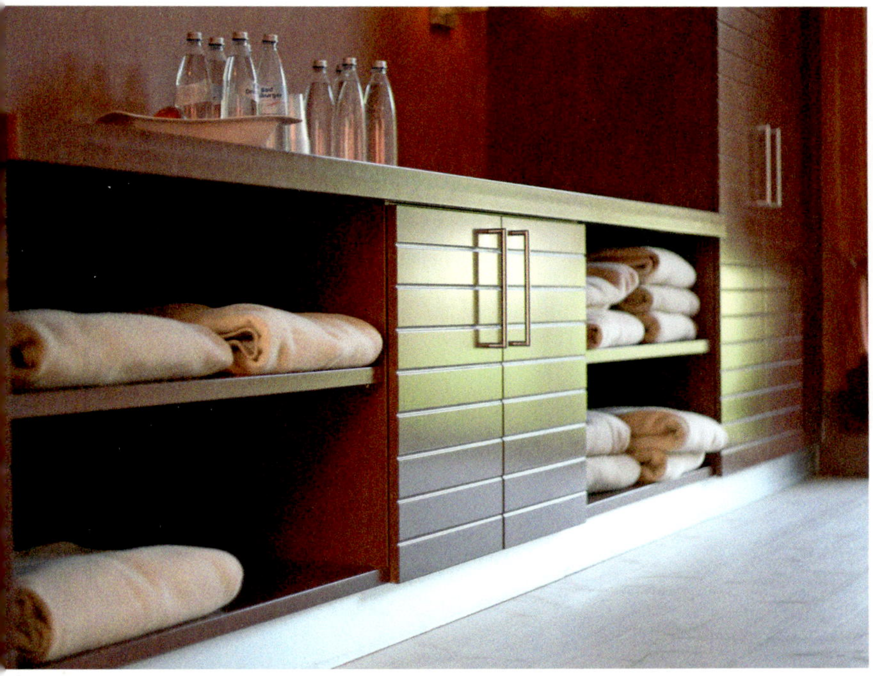
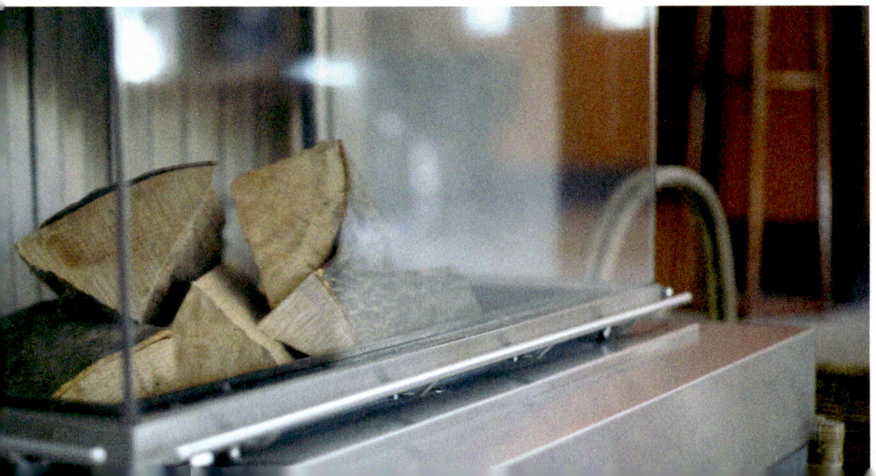
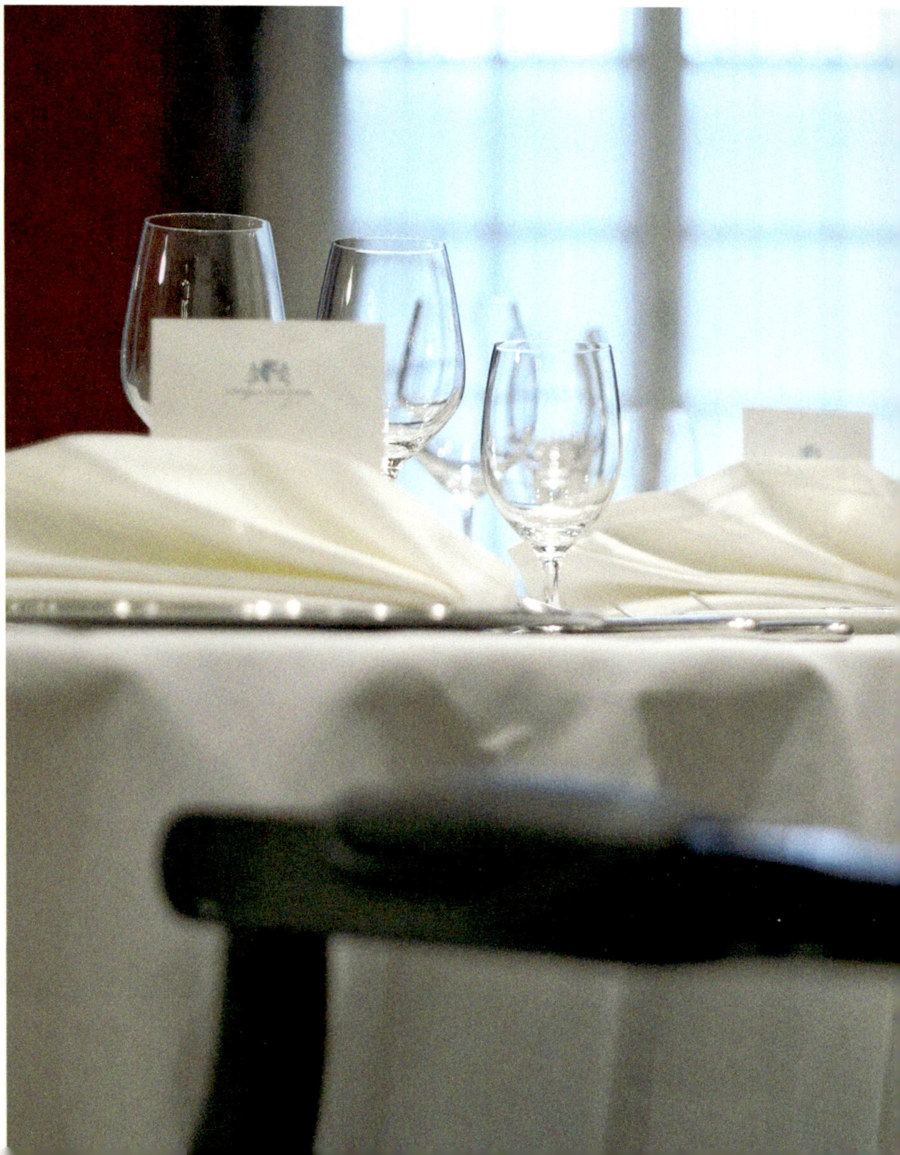

YOUNG BRITISH Empfang | Reception

Mannshohe Vasen gefüllt mit unbeblätterten Kirschzweigen und künstlichen, violetten Orchideen sind so einfach wie prächtig zugleich. Der Kontrast des Rauen mit Edlem bringt den zeitgemäßen, wertig wirkenden Material- und Strukturkontrast. Korrekt ausgearbeitet sind die Trichterformen der floralen Dekoration durch die in sich verankerten und mit Wickeldraht verbundenen Zweige bei gleichzeitiger Transparenz.

EMPFANG RECEPTION

Exceptionally tall vases filled with cherry tree twigs, naked of all leaves, and artificial purple orchids are as understated as they are resplendent. The expensive-looking contrast between the materials and the textures relies on the contrast between noble elegance and roughness. The fluted floral decorations have been precisely formed by skilfully intertwining the twigs in such a way that they hold each other firmly, yet can still be seen through.

YOUNG BRITISH Empfang | Reception

The royal colours of crimson and purple dominate these decorative highlights for the reception area. The arrangement of twigs and sumptuous flowers has been fastened to floral foam, in the large mother-of-pearl vase. The small tabletop variant consists of a decorative gnarled cherry tree twig which has been firmly fastened to a floral foam base, accompanied by artificial magnolias and berry-bearing twigs.

Die royalen Farben Purpur und Violett bestimmen diese Schmuckstücke fürs Entree. Die große Perlmuttvase ist aufstrebend mit Zweigen und Prachtblüten besteckt. Bei der kleinen Variante für den Tisch ziert ein in Steckschaum verankerter, knorriger Kirschzweig mit künstlichen Magnolienblüten und Beerenzweigen.

YOUNG BRITISH Salon | Drawing Room

SALON DRAWING ROOM

Die Pracht der Mohnblüte mit ihrer Größe und sinnlichen Farbe beherrscht hier den Raum. Auf bogenförmig arrangierten Ranken lassen die Blüten sowie die dazu gesteckten Magnolienblätter an prunkvolle Zeiten denken.

The gloriousness of the poppy, its size and sensuous colour, dominates the room. Combined with magnolia leaves and skilfully arranged on an arch of dried vines, they recall grand times.

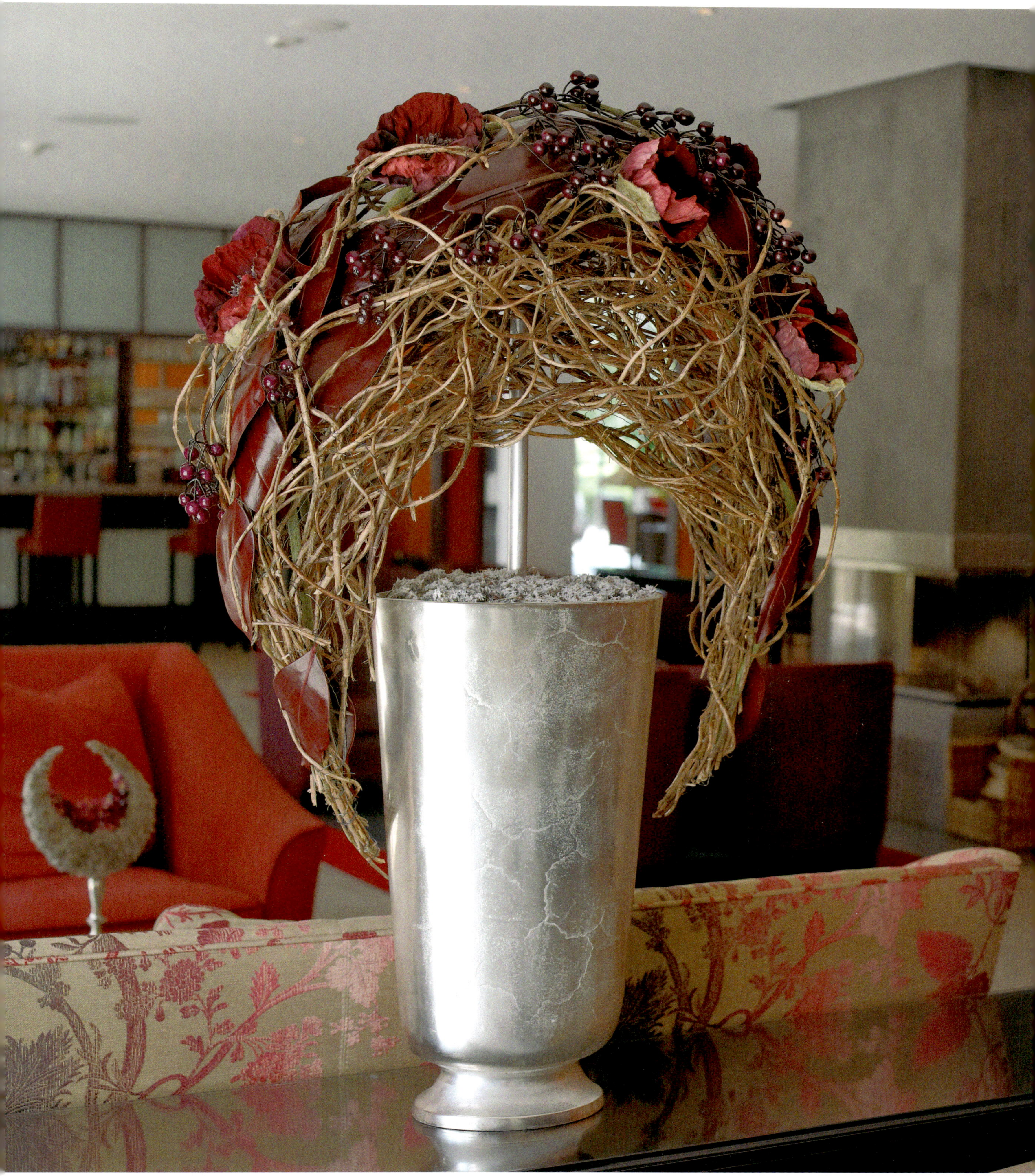

YOUNG BRITISH Salon | Drawing Room

Formale Werkstücke akzentuieren salonartige Räume. Basis bildet jedes Mal eine Heuwulst, auf die die Floralien und Materialien gewickelt oder geklebt sind. Dabei geht vor allem von dunkelroten Magnolienblättern mit den Muschelreihungen bzw. von der grauen Tillandsie die strukturelle Wirkung aus.

TIPP! TIP!

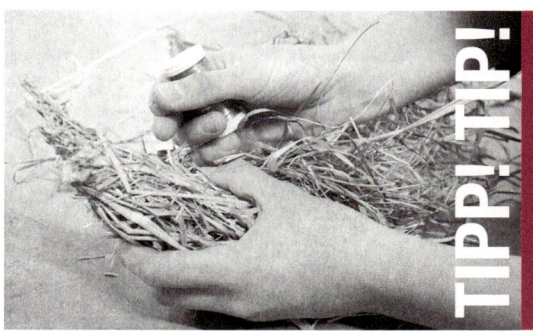

Aus Heu die Form herstellen und mit Wickeldraht fixieren. Dann Tillandsie mit Zierdraht aufwickeln und Floralien ergänzen.

Make the basic shape from hay, secure with binding wire. Then attach tillandsia with decorative wire, finish with floral elements.

Formal arrangements accentuate the drawing room atmosphere of parlour-like rooms. The basis for each of these arrangements is a thick coil of hay. Floral elements and materials are either wrapped around these, or glued on. Textural structure is achieved particularly through the dark red magnolia leaves in combination with rows of shells, and the grey tillandsia.

YOUNG BRITISH Salon | Drawing Room

Kleine Schmuckakzente für die Bar, das Cocktailtischchen oder die Lounge-Ecke. Die Blütenkugel ruht auf einem Metallfuß, die Gefäße mit Blüten sind mit Drahtgespinsten umwoben. Eine Ledermanschette betont das längliche Gefäß mit dunkelroten Blüten.

Decorative accents for the bar, the cocktail table or the lounge corner. The flower-decorated ball rests on a metal stand, jars bearing flowers are enmeshed in woven wire. A leather collar emphasis the longish container holding dark red flowers.

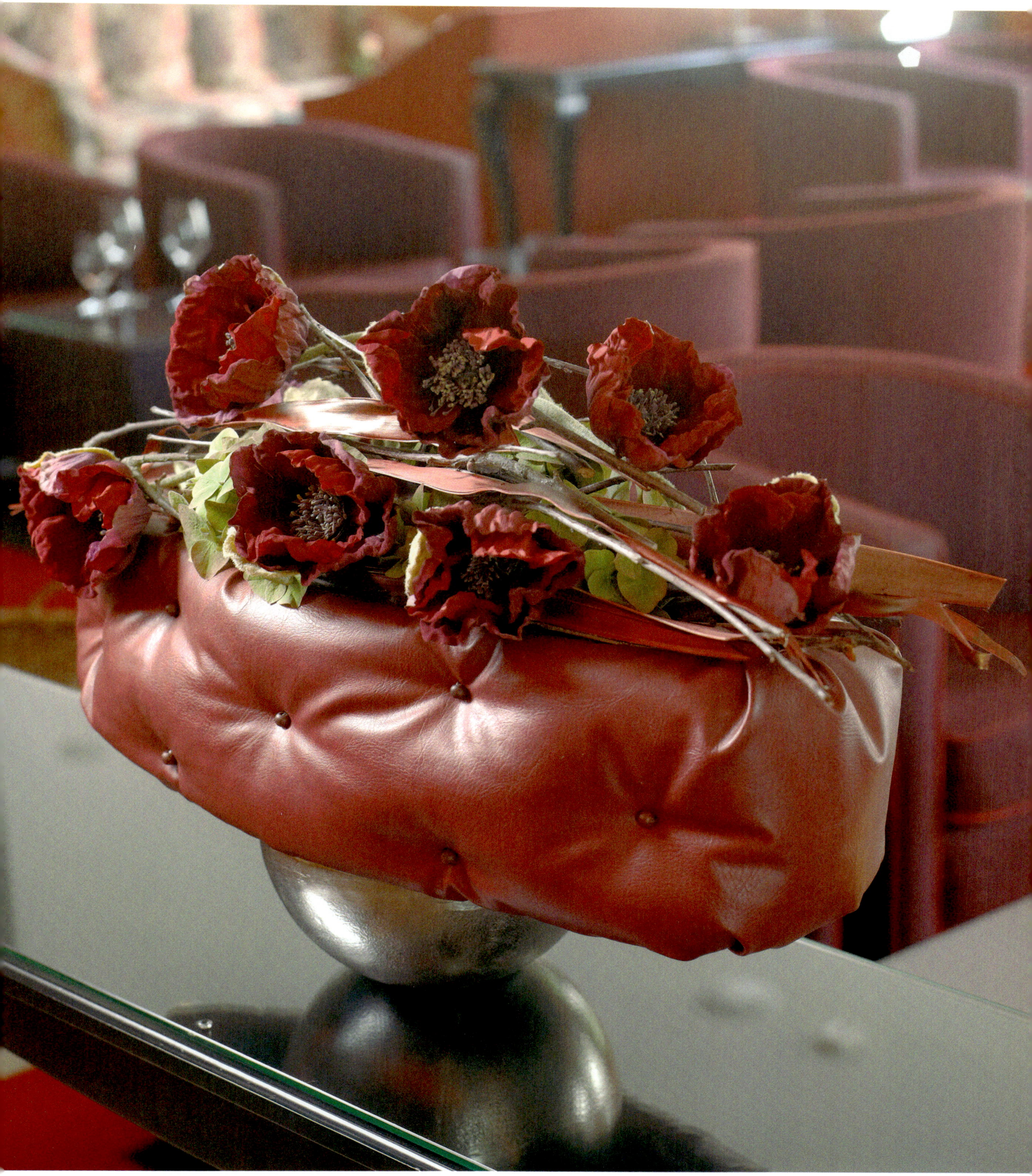

YOUNG BRITISH Festsaal | Ballroom

Blütenschmuck auf hohem, schlankem Sockel wirkt nochmal so prächtig! Basis ist ein Kerzenleuchter, der eine Styroporhalbkugel trägt. Diese ist mit Federn beklebt und im oberen Bereich mit Steckschaum gefüllt zum Bestecken mit allerlei Floralien sowie mit angedrahteten Blättern.

FESTSAAL BALLROOM

Flower arrangements look twice as resplendent when placed on a tall, narrow pedestal! In this case a candle holder bearing a Styrofoam halfsphere. This has been covered in feathers, attached with adhesive, and filled at the top with floral foam to hold various floral elements and leaves attached with the aid of wires.

YOUNG BRITISH Festsaal | Ballroom

Das Füllhorn ist schon seit römischen Zeiten Zeichen der Fülle und Pracht. In schmaler Form auf Ständern gearbeitet, erinnern die schlanken, trichterförmigen und mit Floralien schuppig-gleichmäßig beklebten Stelen daran. Die prachtvolle Blütenfülle aus Pfingstrosen und Beeren und vielem mehr scheint geradezu aus ihnen herauszuquellen. Die Grundformen sind aus Heu gebildet und dann mit dem Blätterkleid versehen worden. Die Blüten sind gesteckt.

Cornucopias have been a symbol of abundance and resplendence since Roman times. They are the inspiration for these slim, fluted stilts, worked in a narrow shape onto stands, then evenly covered in various floral elements arranged in a scaly pattern with the aid of adhesive. The glorious abundance of peonies and berries and a great number of other decorative elements truly seems to spill out of them. The basic shapes have been fashioned from hay, then covered in leaves. The flowers are attached.

YOUNG BRITISH Festsaal | Ballroom

Der Kranz mit den besonderen Kerzenlichtern trägt als Abdeckung einen Kappaplattenring, der mit Stoff umwickelt ist. Floral besteckter Trockenblumensteckschaum ruht auf Kerzenleuchterfüßen. Er ist als Blütenkranz besteckt. Für den Muschelkranz wurde ein mit Band umwickelter Strohrömer mit Muscheln und den Floralien beklebt.

The wreath bearing these unusual votives holds a fabric-covered ring of kapa foamboard mounting. Dry floral foam was decorated with floral elements and rests on the bottom part of candle holders. It has been arranged to resemble a floral wreath. The shell wreath was fashioned from a ribbon-wrapped straw wreath ring, shells and floral elements were attached with glue.

YOUNG BRITISH Wellness | Spa & Bath

WELLNESS SPA & BATH

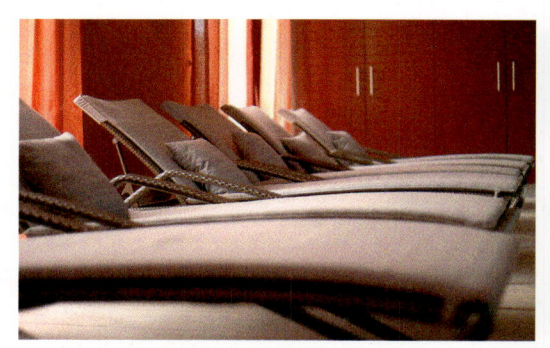

Geheimnisvoll und besonders, eine Ausstrahlung, die zum edlen Spa passt. Die Basis bilden übereinander angeordnete und mit Stäben fixierte Steckschaumziegel, die mit schwarz lackierten Schneckenhäusern beklebt sind.

Mysterious and special, a fitting atmosphere for a luxury spa. The basic shape is achieved by layering floral foam bricks held in place with sticks on top of one another. The snail shells were painted with black gloss paint, then attached to the top of the bricks with glue.

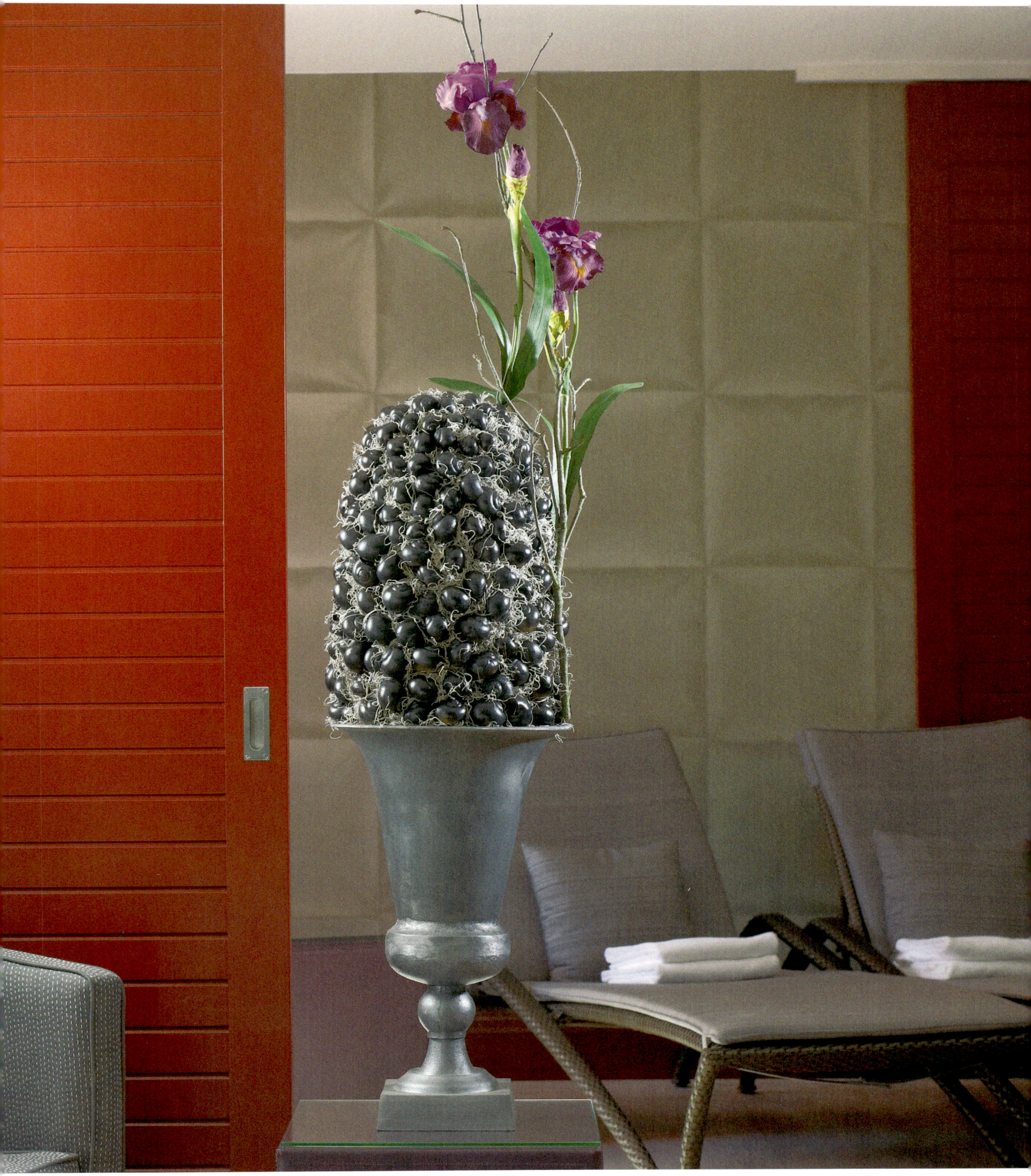

YOUNG BRITISH Wellness | Spa & Bath

Steckschaum ist das konstruktive Geheimnis dieser besonderen Hingucker. Beklebt mit Ungewöhnlichem, wie schwarzen Algen, Flechten und Bleiblech, greifen sie subtil in Materialauswahl und Form das Thema Wasser auf. Lilafarbene Iris toppen die tropfenförmigen Gebilde.

Floral foam is the structural secret of these very special eye-catchers. Unusual elements, such as black algae, lichen and sheet lead, have been attached with adhesive. The choice of materials and their shape subtly picks up on the aquatic theme. Purple iris have been attached to the top of the teardrop-shaped figures.

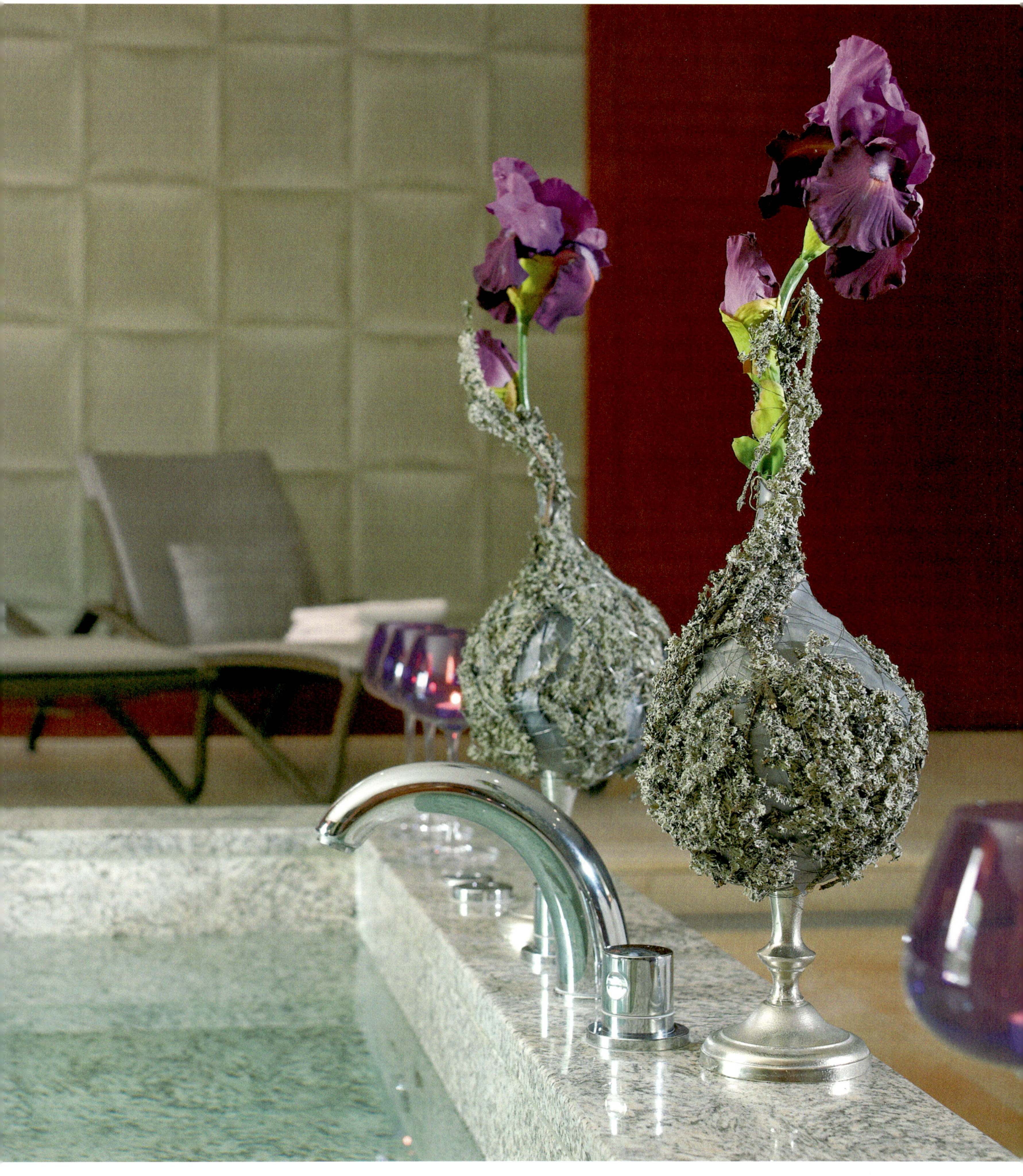

YOUNG BRITISH Wellness | Spa & Bath

The purple-violet colours are repeated in all of the spa rooms. A floral foam extension wrapped in black fabric adds volume and presence to the vase containing beautiful floral elements. Along with attractive deep plate holding a flower arrangement fashioned from various floral elements, shells are also a reminder that everything in these rooms focuses on the elixir of life, water, and its beneficial properties.

Farblich zieht sich das Violett-Lila einheitlich durch die Räume des Spa. Eine mit schwarzem Stoff umwickelte Steckschaumverlängerung gibt dem mit prächtigen Floralien besteckten Gefäß mehr Volumen und Präsenz. Wie auch die aus verschiedenen Floralien zusammengesetzte Blüte in der attraktiven Schale erinnern Muscheln daran, dass sich in diesen Räumen alles ums Lebenselixir Wasser und um seine heilenden Eigenschaften dreht.

TIPP! TIP!

Muschelschalen mit ihren perlmuttfarben schimmernden Innenflächen passen ideal zum Wellness-Thema und lassen sich gut mit Heißkleber am Werkstück fixieren.

Seashells, with their shimmery mother-of-pearl insides, are perfect for a spa-theme, and can simply be glued onto an arrangement with adhesive.

LIGHT LOFT & BUSINESS
COPENHAGEN

Lichtdurchflutet und transparent, modern-architektonisch, technisch bis kühl. Das ist die Atmosphäre von loftartigen Gebäuden, die das Image moderner Büros von Agenturen, Kanzleien oder extravaganter Praxen prägt. Den großzügigen Räumlichkeiten mit viel Glas, Metall oder schlichtem Holz gibt Florales mit grafisch-natürlichem Ausdruck Stil und Lebendigkeit. Rot ist hier die akzentuierende Farbe.

Light-flooded and transparent, modernist architecture, from functional to cool. This loft-style atmosphere characterises agencies, lawyer's or extravagant doctor's offices with a contemporary image. Floral arrangements with a graphics inspired, natural style add style and liveliness to generously proportioned sets of rooms featuring plenty of glass, metal or plain wood; red is the accentuating colour.

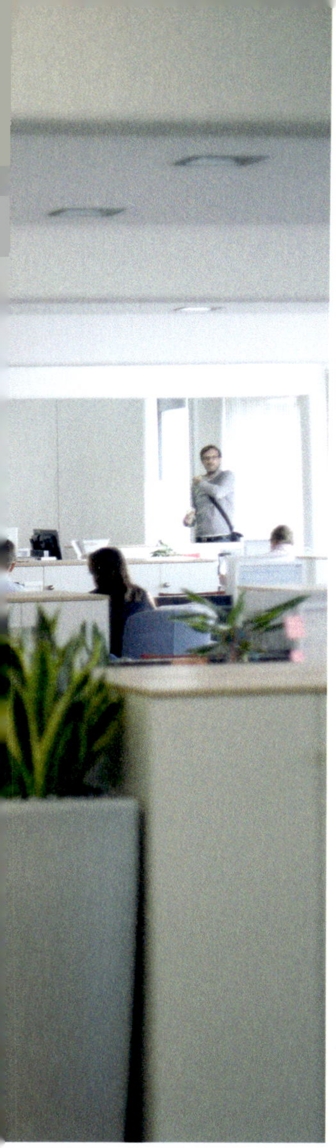
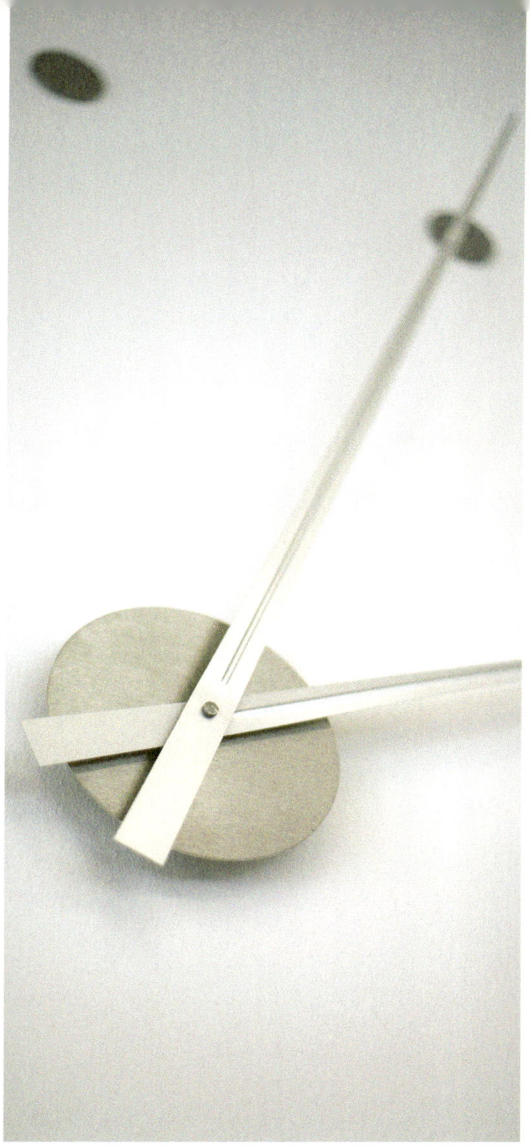
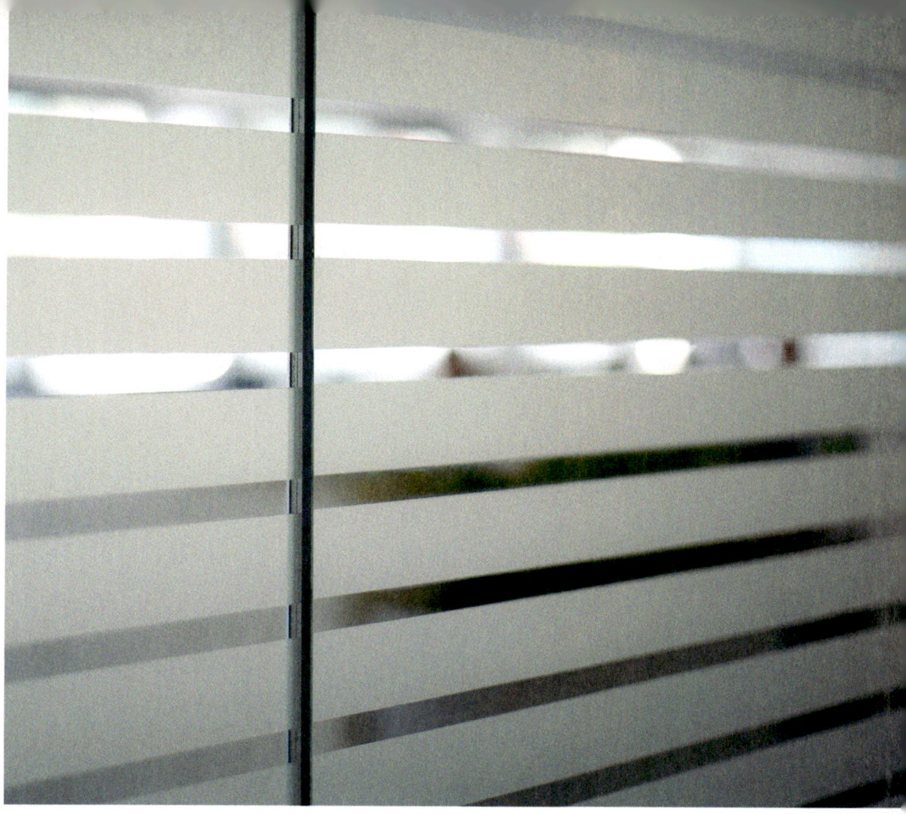
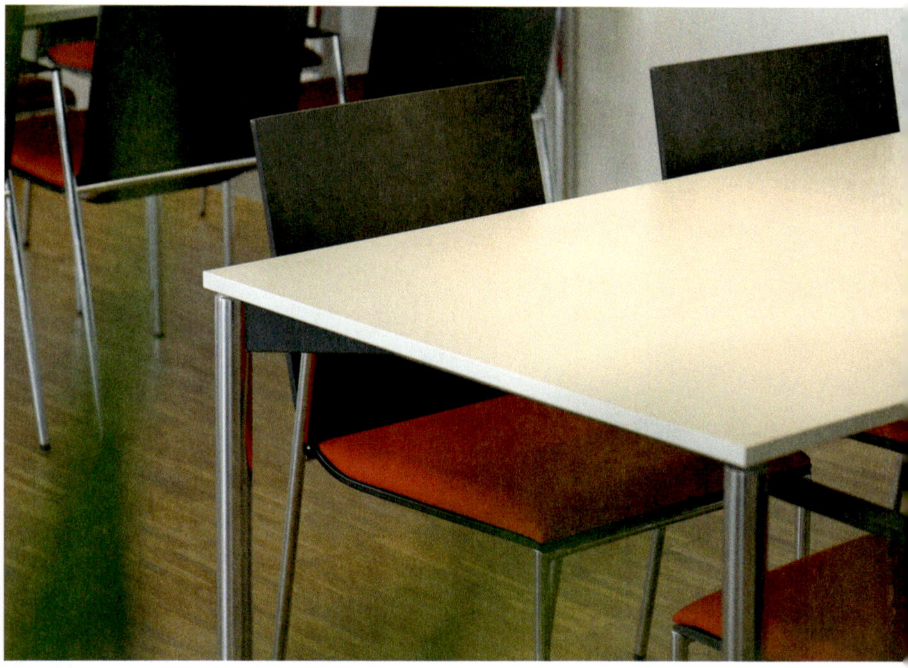
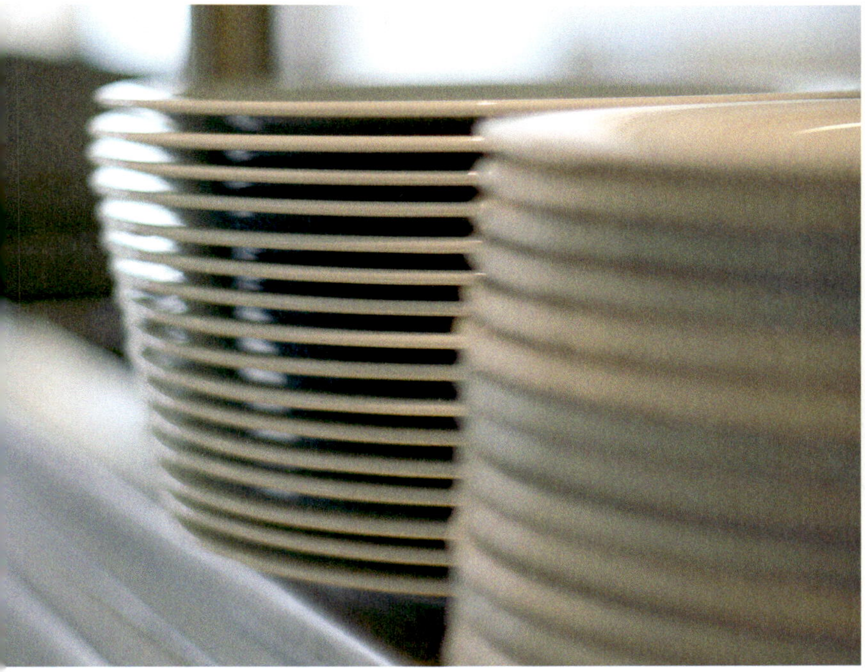
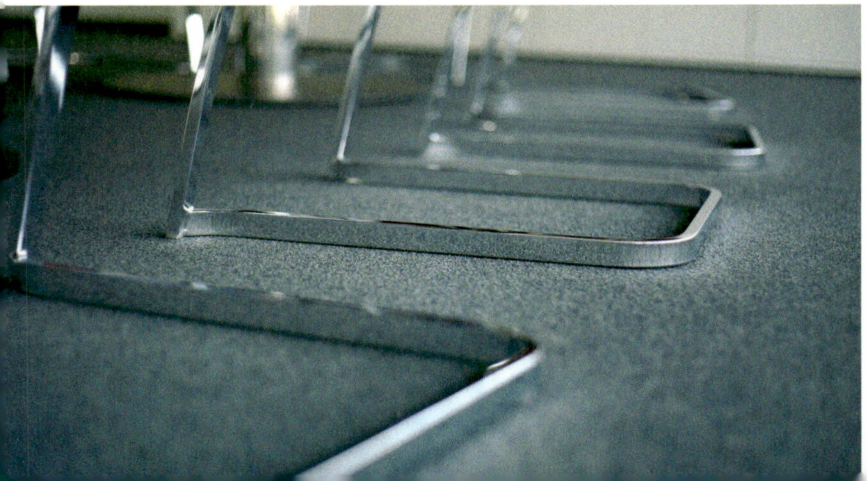
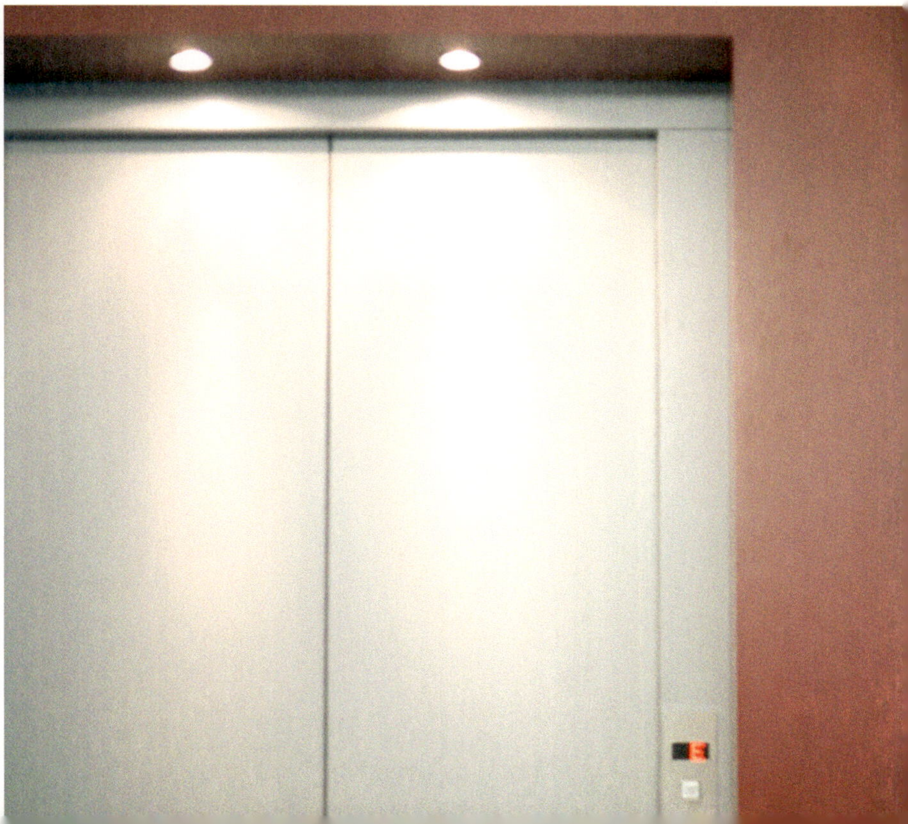

LIGHT COPENHAGEN Entree | Foyer

ENTREE FOYER

Ein herzlicher Willkommensgruß soll es sein, der nicht stört bei der Anmeldung und den Aktivitäten, die sich mit dem Empfangstresen verbinden. Das quaderförmige und sich damit in der raumgreifenden Wirkung beschränkende Werkstück ist ideal und in der paarweisen Anordnung – sofern Platz vorhanden – doppelt attraktiv. Dazu wird das Gerüst aus einzelnen groben, senkrecht aneinander fixierten Birkenstäben in die rechteckige Schieferschale geklemmt und die künstlichen Blüten dazwischen arrangiert. Zum Schluss die Schale mit Sand auffüllen.

It should be a warm welcome which does not get in the way of registration or other activities dealt with at the reception counter. Limited space is needed for these rectangular, cubic designs, making them perfect for counters; they are twice as attractive in pairs – provided there is sufficient space for two. For this arrangement, a skeleton made of single rough birch twigs which have been vertically attached to each other is wedged into a slate bowl; the artificial flowers are inserted in between. To finish, fill the bowl with sand.

LIGHT COPENHAGEN Entree | Foyer

Practice, agency or lawyer's office waiting rooms are a reflection of the corporate image. Clients or patients should therefore enjoy their stay there, made more pleasant by attractive floral arrangements. The red floor vase with fly wire accent and vertically inserted artificial flowers contrasts lovely with the birch branches and grasses. The arrangement of four glass jars on the side table catches the eye. The colour of the red ribbon wrapped around the jars reflects the colour of the matching larger floor vase, the birch bark wrapped around the floral foam cube reflects the materials used in the large design.

Wartezonen von Praxen, Agenturen oder Kanzleien sind ein Aushängeschild fürs Unternehmen. Insofern sollte man hier den Klienten oder Patienten eine blumig-freundliche Verweilzeit bieten. Ein Farbtupfer mit Anziehungskraft ist das rote Bodengefäß mit Fliegendrahtakzent und senkrecht eingesteckten, künstlichen Blumen zu Birkenstäben und Gräsern. Auf dem Beistelltisch fällt der Blick auf das Glas-Quartett. Die rote Bandumwicklung ist die farbliche, die Umwicklung des Steckwürfels mit Birkenrinde die materialbezogene Entsprechung zum korrespondierenden Großgefäß.

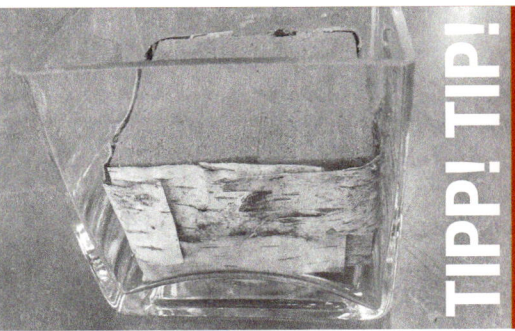

TIPP! TIP!

Zum Kaschieren des Steckschaums passend geschnittene Rindenstreifen mit Heißkleber um den Würfel kleben. Der Würfel sollte nicht zu knapp im Glaskubus sitzen.

To hide the floral foam, glue birch bark, cut to size, around the floral foam cubes with hot glue. The cubes should not be wedged too tightly into the glass cubes.

LIGHT COPENHAGEN Entree | Foyer

Birkenrinde bringt Natürlichkeit im kühlen, loftartigen Raumambiente. Unterschiedlich große Rindenquadrate kaschieren die Seitenflächen des Steckschaumwürfels in den Glaskuben. Die in großen, quaderförmigen Gefäßen eingestellten Äste verstärken den Aspekt des natürlichen Gegenpols.

Birch bark adds naturalness to a cool, loft-style interior. Bark squares in various sizes hide the sides of the floral foam cubes inside the glass cubes. The branches standing upright in large, rectangular containers enhance the impression of a natural antipole.

TIPP! TIP!

Mit Draht und Tape lassen sich auf natürlich wirkende Art Blumenstiele verlängern. Dazu Steckdraht knicken, mit einer Zange an den Stiel drücken und den Übergang mit Klebeband umwickeln.

Flower stems can be extended in a way that looks natural by using wire and tape. To achieve this, bend fixing wire, attach to the stem using pliers, then wrap tape around where they meet.

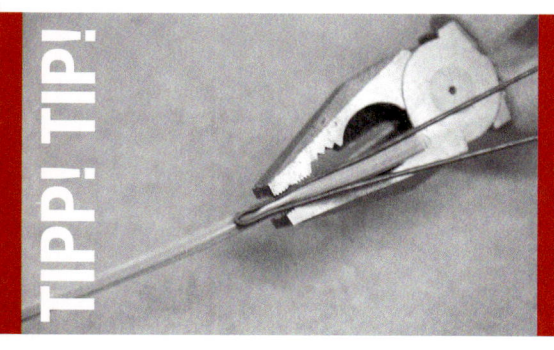

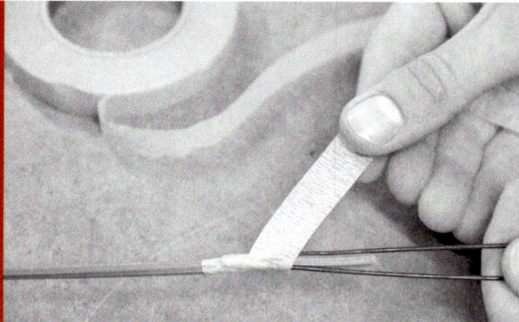

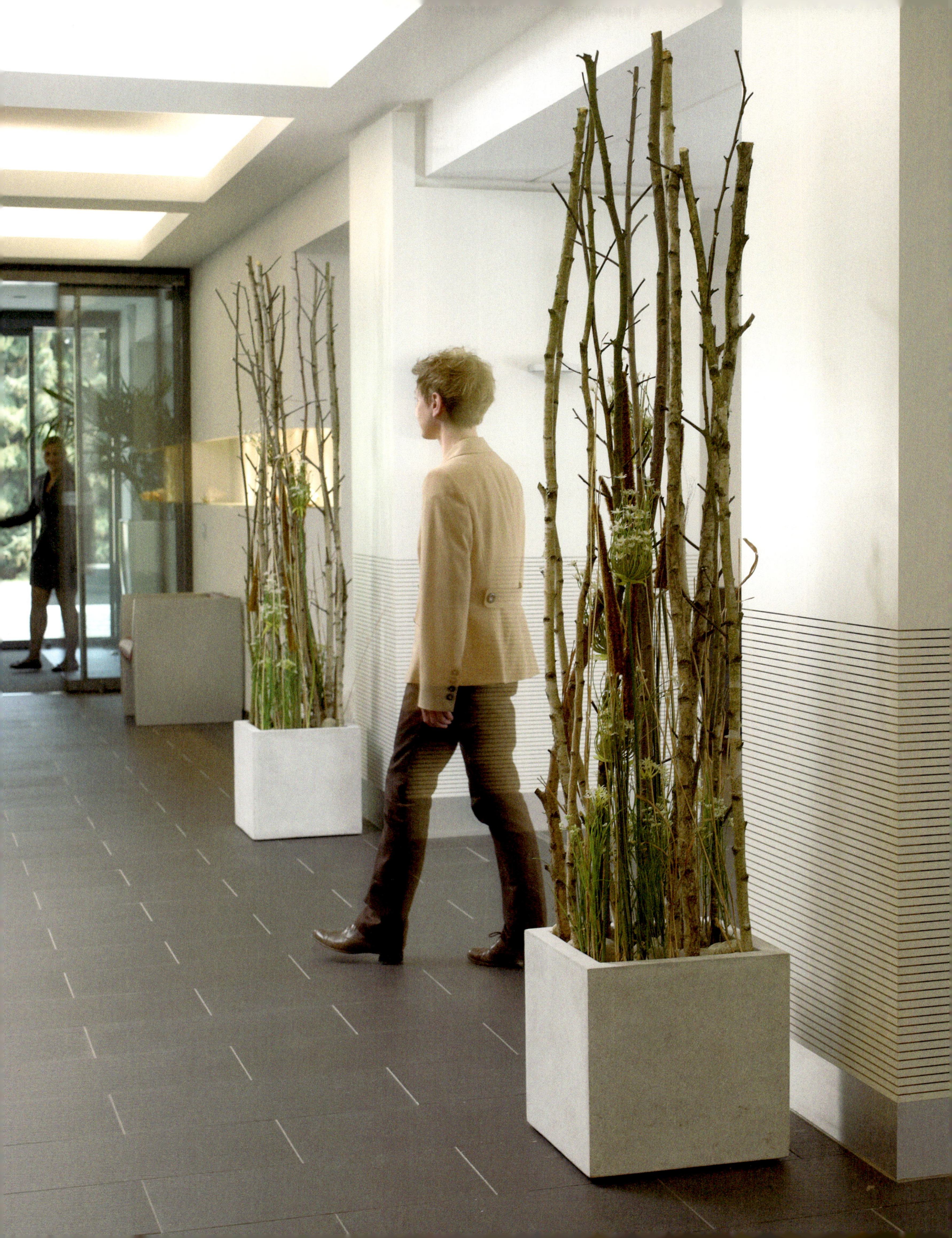

LIGHT COPENHAGEN Konferenzraum | Meeting Room

Die Transparenz und architektonische Nuance des Gebäudes greift diese Tischdekoration im Konferenzraum auf. Große Blüten werden zusammen mit einem locker gewundenen Drahtseil, den rund gelegten Blumenstielen sowie Rindenstreifenwicklungen in die Glaswannen gelegt oder geklemmt. Die sich überall durchziehende Firmenfarbe Bordeauxrot nimmt das entsprechend gefärbte und hinzugesteckte Strelitzienblatt auf, passend zu der Konferenzraumbestuhlung.

KONFERENZRAUM MEETING ROOM

This table decoration in the meeting rooms picks up on the building's transparency and architectural nuances. Large flowers are placed in or wedged into the glass containers, together with a loosely wound coil of piano wire, coiled flower stems and coiled strips of bark. The correspondingly dyed and added leaf of a bird-of-paradise flower adds a touch of claret, the corporate colour, also matched by the meeting room chairs' fabric.

LIGHT COPENHAGEN Konferenzraum | Meeting Room

Die blumige Überwucherung der mit Stahlseilschlaufen versehenen Betonplatte als Mittelpunkt auf dem Besprechungstisch sowie die leichten, filigranen Kokons aus Reedstäben und Draht mit künstlichen Blüten unterstreichen die Modernität der Räume.

The flower-covered concrete slab decorated with looped steel wire is the focus of the meeting room table, accentuating the contemporariness of the rooms, as do the light, filigree cocoons made from reeds and artificial flowers.

TIPP! TIP!

Betonmasse in einen mit Folie ausgelegten Holzrahmen gießen. Drahtbögen hinzu stecken, aushärten lassen. Werkstück mit Filzfüßen versehen.

Pour concrete into a wooden frame lined with foil. Insert wire loops, let it harden. Fasten felt stands underneath.

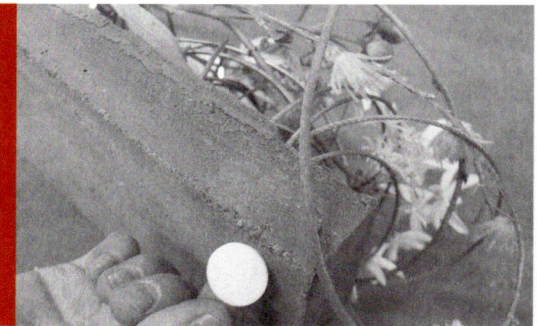

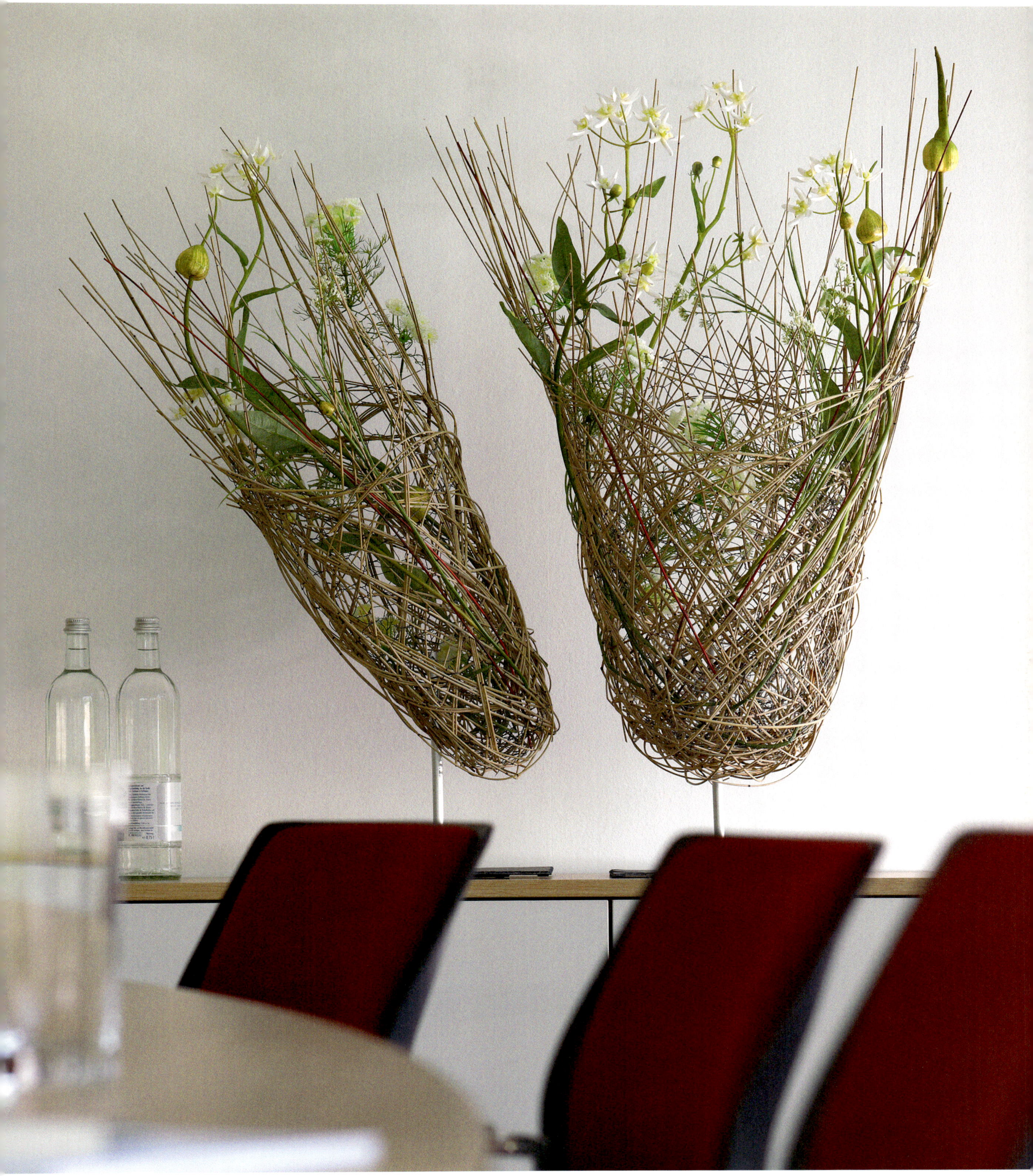

LIGHT COPENHAGEN Büro | Office

BÜRO OFFICE

Längs seitlich am Arbeitsplatz lassen sich gereihte Dekorationen gut platzieren. In den Betonkuben dienen gebündelte Reedstäbe als Steckbasen, in den Glaswannen weißer Sand. Ketten aus aneinander getackerten Birkenrindenringen bringen spielerische Leichtigkeit.

A row of floral decorations looks good placed at the side of the workspace. Bundled reeds inserted in concrete serve as the basis for this design, the glass containers have been filled with white sand. Chains made from birch bark rings, stapled together, add a touch of playfulness.

TIPP! TIP!

Für die perfekte Schnittflächen-Ebene Reedstäbe-Abschnitte in den Steckschaum mit Sandabdeckung stecken. Dann Brett auflegen und leicht mit dem Hammer draufschlagen, so bekommen alle die gleiche Länge!

To achieve a perfectly level edge, insert cut reeds into the sand-covered floral foam. Then place a board on top and hit lightly with a hammer – that way, they will all have the same length!

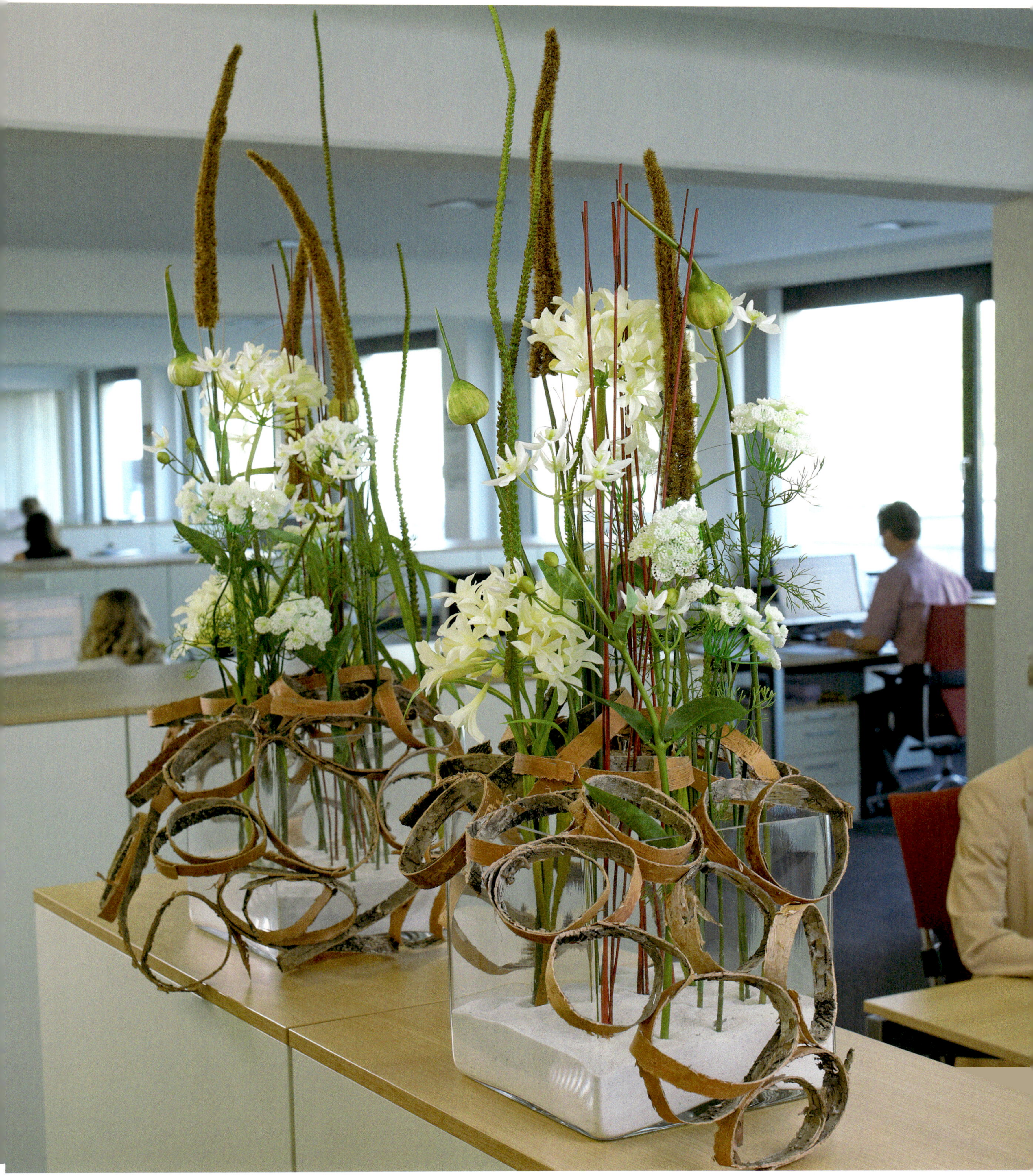

LIGHT COPENHAGEN Kantine | Canteen

Hygienisch muss es hier zugehen und dekorativ zugleich. Rechteckige, längliche Gefäße sind auf Kantinentischen platzsparend, denn beidseitig müssen Essenstabletts noch Platz finden. Im Schiefergefäß sind die senkrecht eingeschichteten Filz- und Rindenstücke mit den Blüten verklebt. In den Betongefäßen wird nach dem Bestecken flüssiger Gips zur dauerhaften Fixierung eingefüllt.

KANTINE CANTEEN

Here, hygiene must be considered alongside decoration. Rectangular, longish containers save space on canteen tables, leaving enough place for food trays. Inside the slate container, vertically inserted layers of pieces of felt and bark have been glued to the flowers. Once the flowers have been arranged, the concrete containers are filled with liquid plaster for permanent fixing.

TIPP! TIP!

Gefäß mit Steckschaum versehen und mit Floralien bestecken. Zum Schluss dünne Schicht Gips eingießen, fest werden lassen und mit Sand bedecken.

Place floral foam in container and arrange flowers. Finish off by pouring in a thin layer of plaster, let harden and cover with sand.

LIGHT COPENHAGEN Waschraum | Cloakroom

WASCHRAUM CLOAKROOM

Glas und Beton passen auch in den Sanitärbereich; künstliche Blüten und Birkenholz sind prädestiniert für diese Räume. Ein Streifen Hasendraht sowie Drahtgaze geben dem Arrangement im Glaskubus sowohl eine technische Nuancierung als auch den Floralien Halt und die benötigte Standfestigkeit. Gleiche Funktion haben auch die Birkenzweige beim Betonzylinder; sie fußen in Steckschaum. Alles umkränzt der aufgeklebte Birkenrindenstreifen.

Glass and concrete are also suitable for the cloakrooms; artificial flowers and birch bark are predestined for these rooms. Chicken wire and wire gauze add a functional note to the arrangement in the glass cube, as well as adding stability and holding the flowers. The birch twigs in the concrete cylinders fulfil the same function, their base being floral foam. The arrangement is encircled by a strip of glued-on birch bark.

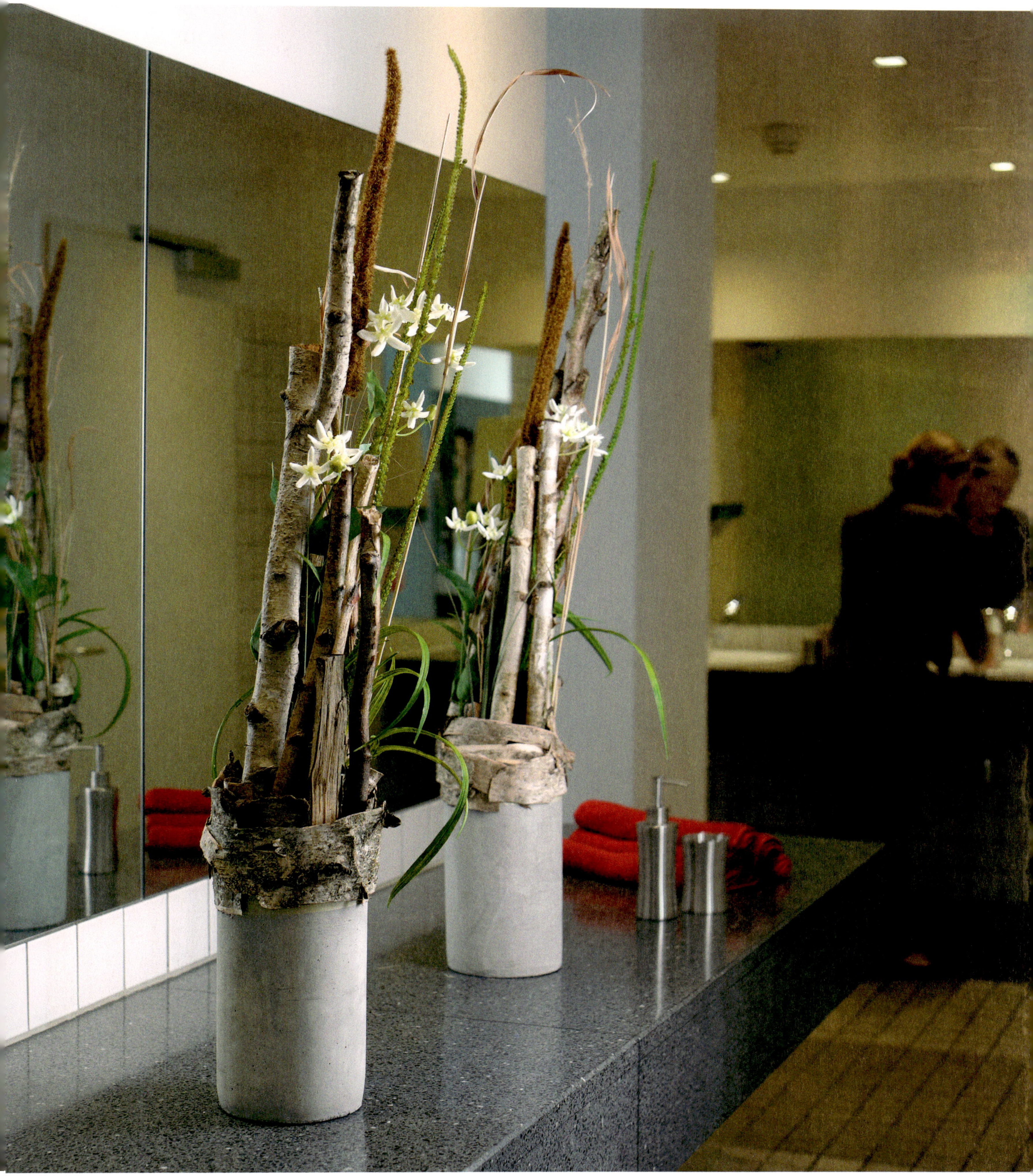

LIGHT COPENHAGEN Waschraum | Cloakroom

Fine-meshed wire gauze adds a special touch to this large floor vase – and again, a functional note. The collar is given volume through bracing wire loops, covered by strips of wire mesh. The final layer is wire fabric. The fabric can easily be given the desired shape and structure by pushing and pulling. This allows the forming of a cone-like hollow in the centre of the vase to hold the flowers, which are placed into it to resemble a wreath. An exciting interior is revealed to anyone looking into the vase from above.

Feinmaschige Drahtgaze gibt diesem großen Bodengefäß die besondere – und wiederum – technische Note. Volumen erhält die Manschette durch Spanndrahtbögen, über die Maschendrahtstreifen gelegt und die schließlich mit dem Drahtgewebe bedeckt werden. Das Gewebe wird durch Zurechtdrücken in die gewünschte Form und Struktur gebracht. So wird eine trichterähnliche Vertiefung in der Mitte des Gefäßes gestaltet, die Floralien kranzförmig hineingelegt, so dass sich beim Blick in die Tiefe des Gefäßes dem Betrachter eine spannende Innenansicht offenbart.

COSY RESTAURANT
BRUXELLES

Räume mit Wohlfühlcharakter, voller Sinnlichkeit und gelebter Geselligkeit, prägen Orte der Gastronomie. Holz, Steinwände oder Mauerwerk, dazu Blumengestecke, Kränze oder Girlanden, geben diesem Ambiente Charakter. Sie sind mit ihrer natürlichen Ausstrahlung mehr als nur einladender Willkommensgruß, nämlich auch Ausdruck eines ländlich-floralen Selbstverständnisses.

Restaurants are rooms distinguished by their comfort-character, full of joie de vivre and companionableness. Wood, stone walls or exposed brickwork and floral arrangements such as wreaths or garlands add to this atmosphere's character. With their natural vibrancy, they are more than just a welcoming gesture; they are the floral expression of a country-inspired self-image.

Getränke-Karte

COSY BRUXELLES Eingang | Entrance

EINGANG ENTRANCE

Im rustikalen Interieur mit Ziegelsteinboden und Holzmobiliar begrüßen florale Bäumchen die Gäste. Die Trockenfloralien stecken in Steckschaumzylindern, die auf den Stab geklebt sind. Der Wollkragen der Blütentuffs in den steinernen Gefäßen sind aus Filzschnur gehäkelt.

In this rustic interior setting complete with brick floors and wooden furniture, guests are greeted by small floral trees. Dried flowers and greenery are inserted into floral foam cylinders which are glued to a wooden staff. The woolly collars of the tufts of flowers in the stone jars have been crocheted using felt twine.

COSY BRUXELLES Gaststube | Bar Parlour

Wo früher Würste und Speck trockneten, zieren jetzt Trockenblumenbündel. Um dem Metallring mehr Präsenz zu geben, wird er zusätzlich mit einem dicken Heukranz versehen. Dazu einen Weidenring erst mit Zeitungspapier, dann mit Heu bewickeln. Knorrige, verholzte Efeuranken bilden das stelzenartige Gestell, das zwei mit Rosenblüten beklebte Kugeln trägt. Die Unterseiten der Steckschaumkugeln sind mit Blättern besteckt.

GASTSTUBE BAR PARLOUR

Bunches of dried flowers are now decoratively attached where sausages and bacon were once hung to cure. To underline its presence, a thick layer of hay covers the metal wreath. To make, wrap newspaper around a willow wreath ring, then cover with hay. Gnarled, lignified strands of ivy form the stilt-like base supporting two balls, covered in glued-on rose buds. Leaves have been glued to the lower halves of the floral foam balls in a scaly pattern.

COSY BRUXELLES Gaststube | Bar Parlour

Palmfaserkranz auf Holzstumpf oder Flechtzopf mit Heuseele, künstliche Blüten und Früchte leuchten dekorativ neben farbigen Blättern und wolligen Accessoires. Auch Kokosfaser oder raues Paketband sind Bestandteile, die materialgerecht in dieses Ambiente passen.

Palm fibre wreath on a small wooden stump or braided garland with a hay base, artificial fruit and flowers glow decoratively next to colourful leaves and woolly accessories. Coir or rough parcel ribbon are also elements with material characteristics perfectly suited to this atmosphere.

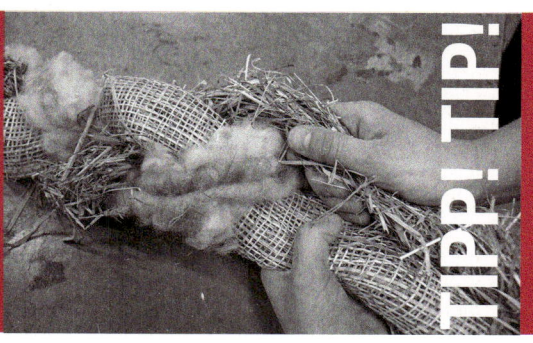

TIPP! TIP!

Ein Strang aus Heu, ein Strang aus Jute und einer aus Flauschbändern werden für den Zopf miteinander verflochten.

One skein of hay, one skein of jute and one of fluffy ribbon are intertwined to make the braided garland.

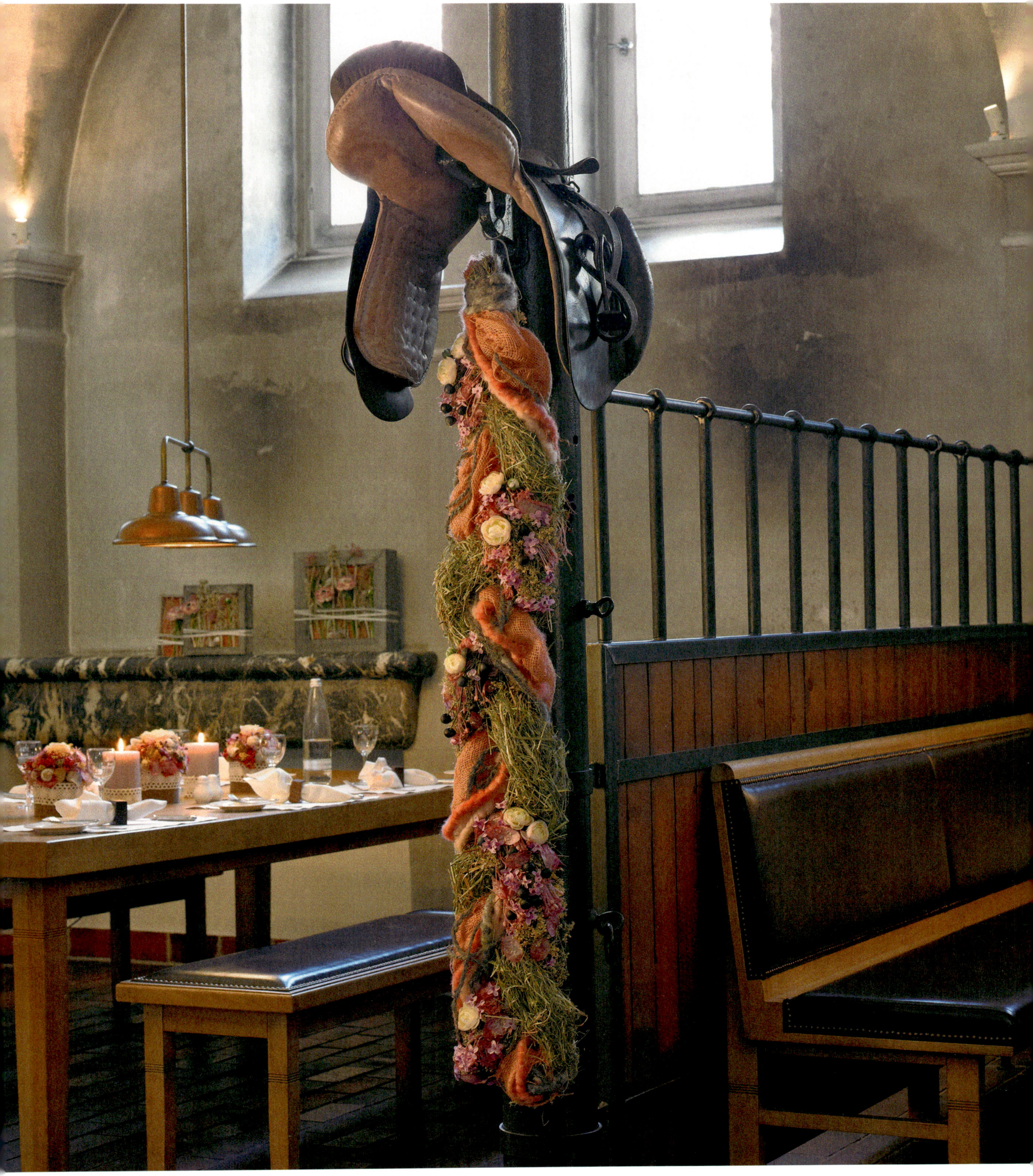

COSY BRUXELLES Gaststube | Bar Parlour

Nicht nur der Duft, auch die Farbe und die Struktur von Heu gehören zum ländlich-rustikalen Ambiente. Das Trockengras wird dick auf einen Holzstumpf gewickelt und die Blüten – egal ob größer oder kleinteiliger – nestartig mit Steckschaum eingearbeitet.

Not only the fragrance, but also the colour and structure of hay are part of a rustic country atmosphere. Dried grass is wrapped thickly around a wooden stump and flowers – both smaller elements and larger heads – are attached, nest-like, with the aid of floral foam.

TIPP! TIP!

Für die Grundform Holzklotz mit Steckschaum verlängern. Anschließend mithilfe von Schmuckdraht mit Heu bewickeln.

To get the basic shape, extend the wooden stump with floral foam, then wrap the hay around it with decorative wire.

COSY BRUXELLES Kaminecke | Inglenook

KAMINECKE INGLENOOK

Tabletts werden zu floralen Wandbildern. Dazu mit Jutematte auslegen, Trockenfloralien sowie künstliche Blüten aufkleben und mit Spitze und Draht umwickeln. Beim Wandkranz füllt ein aus Pappe geschnittener Kreis die Kranzöffnung. Hierauf Steckschaum kleben und die Floralien einstecken.

Trays are turned into floral wall-hangings. To make, line with jute mats, then glue on dried flowers and greenery and artificial flowers. Finish by tying lace ribbons and wire around the tray. The inside of the wreath on the wall has been lined with a circle cut from cardboard. Glue floral foam onto this and insert floral decorations.

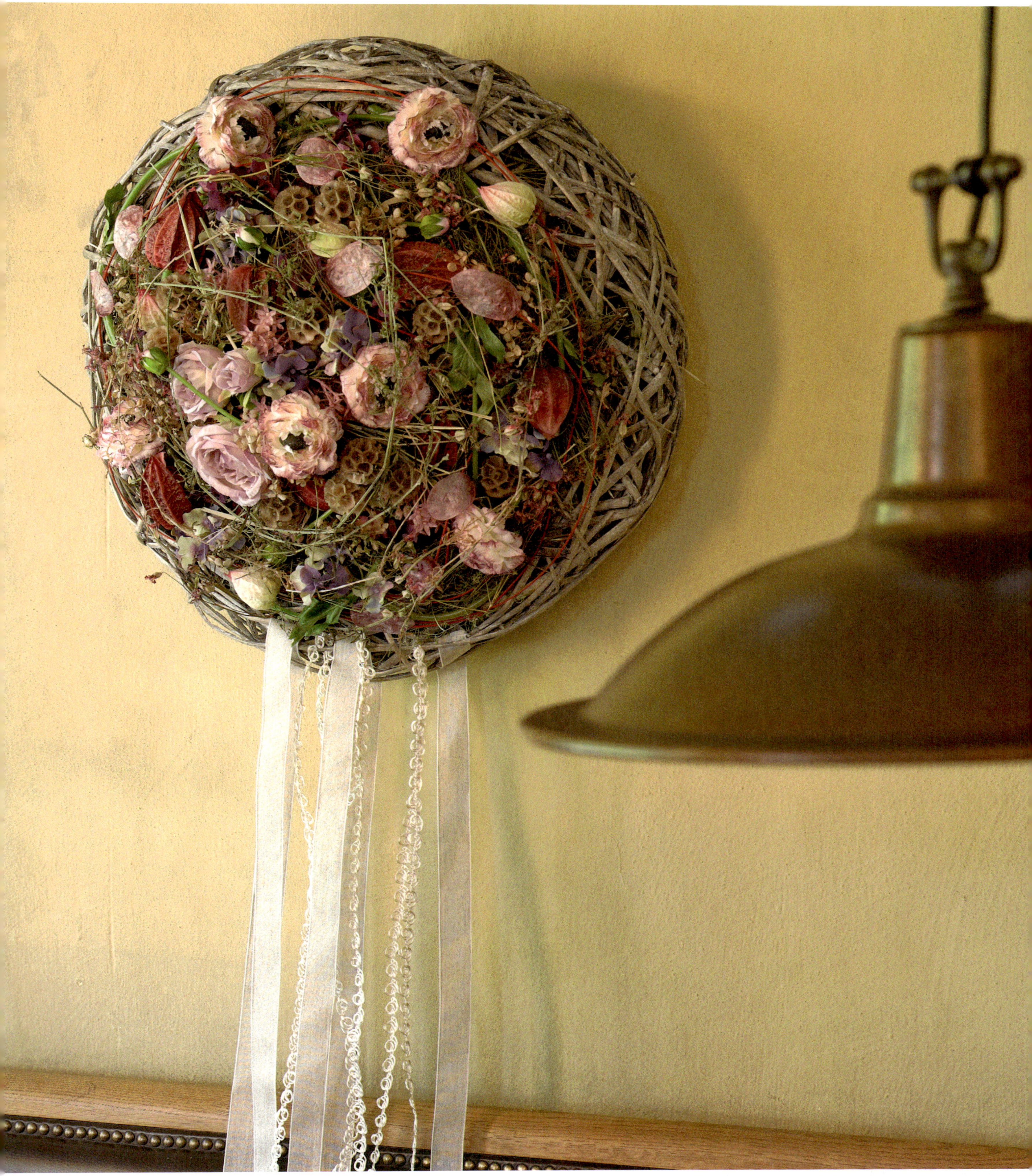

COSY BRUXELLES Büfett | Buffet

Little niches accentuated with floral decorations give this restaurant its charm. The counter decoration was made by extending the container with floral foam wrapped in fern, then the flowers were inserted at the top. A wreath decorates the mantelpiece. To make, glue two crocheted braids fashioned from wool to a cardboard disc, and add floral elements around the centre. Twigs support floral foam bricks wrapped in hay to which strips of fabric have been glued form the basis for this flower arrangement.

Kleine Nischen floral akzentuiert, machen diese Lokalität so liebenswert. Für den Tresenschmuck wird das Gefäß mit Farn umwickeltem Steckschaum verlängert und die Blüten oben eingesteckt. Ein Kranz ziert das Kaminsims. Dazu eine Pappscheibe mit zwei gehäkelten Wollzöpfen sowie mittig eingearbeiteten Floralien bekleben. Die auf Astfüße gestellten Steckschaumziegel sind mit Heu umwickelt und mit Stoff beklebt sowie mit Blüten besteckt.

BÜFETT BUFFET

COSY BRUXELLES Büfett | Buffet

Ein liebliche, ländlich-bäuerlich inspirierte Welt eröffnet sich mit diesem Etagerenschmuck: Geliebtes, Gesammeltes, Schönes verbindet sich zu dekorativer Anmutung. Im Detail sind es Gefäße, wie die Craquelee-Vase, die mit einem Geschirrtuch umlegten, ländlichen Blütenschmuck birgt. Das Gefäß mit Flechtoberfläche wird von einem Strickrand geschmückt sowie einem Edelweiß auf einer Heukugel.

This three-tiered étagère creates a lovely, rustic country-style inspired look. Much-loved pieces, collectibles and pretty things are combined to great decorative effect. A closer look reveals various jars and containers, such as the crackle-glaze vase with a tea towel collar holding country-style floral decorations. The container with the woven outer is decorated with a knitted collar and an edelweiss on a hay ball.

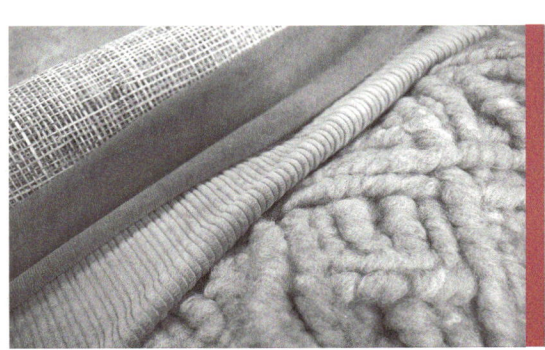

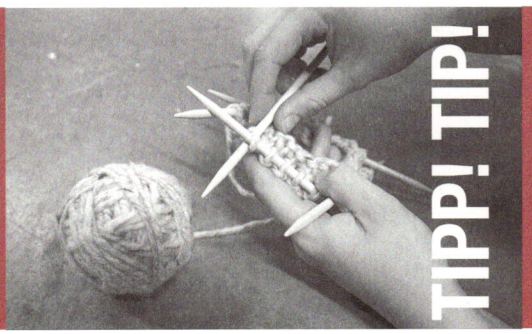

TIPP! TIP!

Der Strickrand ist schnell gemacht: Dicke Wolle, dicke Stricknadeln und die Anleitung für ein Pulloverärmelbündchen. Nach fünf Runden abketten und über den Topf stülpen.

The knitted collar is easy to make: chunky wool, a thick pair of knitting needles, just follow the instructions for jumper sleeve cuffs. Cast off after five rounds and put over the pot.

COSY BRUXELLES Tischdekoration | Table Sets

Lace ribbon that could have come straight from grandma's trousseau. It decorates the pillar candles, but also the fabric-covered floral foam cylinders. To finish, a compact half-round arrangement of dried flowers and snail shells attached to wires is either inserted or glued on, crowned by a beautiful rose.

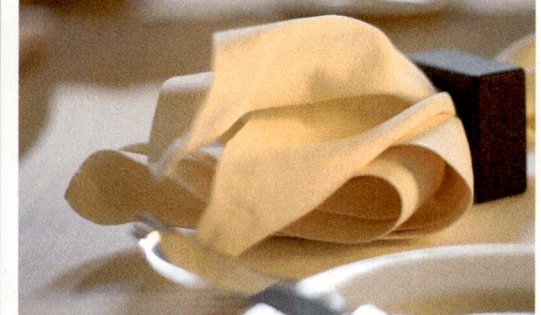

TISCHDEKO TABLE SETS

Spitzenband, wie es sich in Omas Wäschetruhe finden lässt. Dieses ziert Stumpenkerzen, aber auch die mit Stoff umwickelten Steckschaumzylinder. Anschließend werden die Trockenfloralien sowie angedrahtete Schneckenhäuser rundlich-kompakt eingesteckt oder aufgeklebt. Oben thront eine wunderbare Rosenblüte.

COSY BRUXELLES Tischdekoration | Table Sets

Kleine Gestecke bilden den Mittelpunkt auf den schlichten Holztischen. Ob in Craquelee-Vasen oder auf Holzstümpfe gearbeitet, ihre floralen Ausgestaltungen passen zueinander, so dass man sie in Mengen beliebig miteinander kombinieren kann. Geschirrtücher mit traditioneller Musterung umgeben die Blütenarrangements aus künstlichen und getrockneten Bestandteilen.

Small arrangements are a focus on plain wooden tables. Whether in crackle-glazed vases or attached to wooden stumps, their floral finishes match, so random numbers of them can be combined. Tea towels with traditional patterns form collars for the flower arrangements featuring artificial and dried elements.

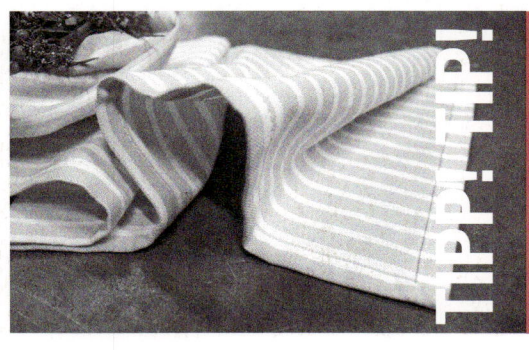

TIPP! TIP!

Floristik mit Textilien eine ländliche Note zu geben, ist zur Zeit aktuell und wirkt füllig zugleich! Verwendet man dazu Küchentücher, lassen sie sich später weiter verwenden.

Adding fabrics to floral arrangements for a touch of country-style is absolutely contemporary and yet opulent! If waiting or glass cloths are used, they can be reused for their original purpose later on.

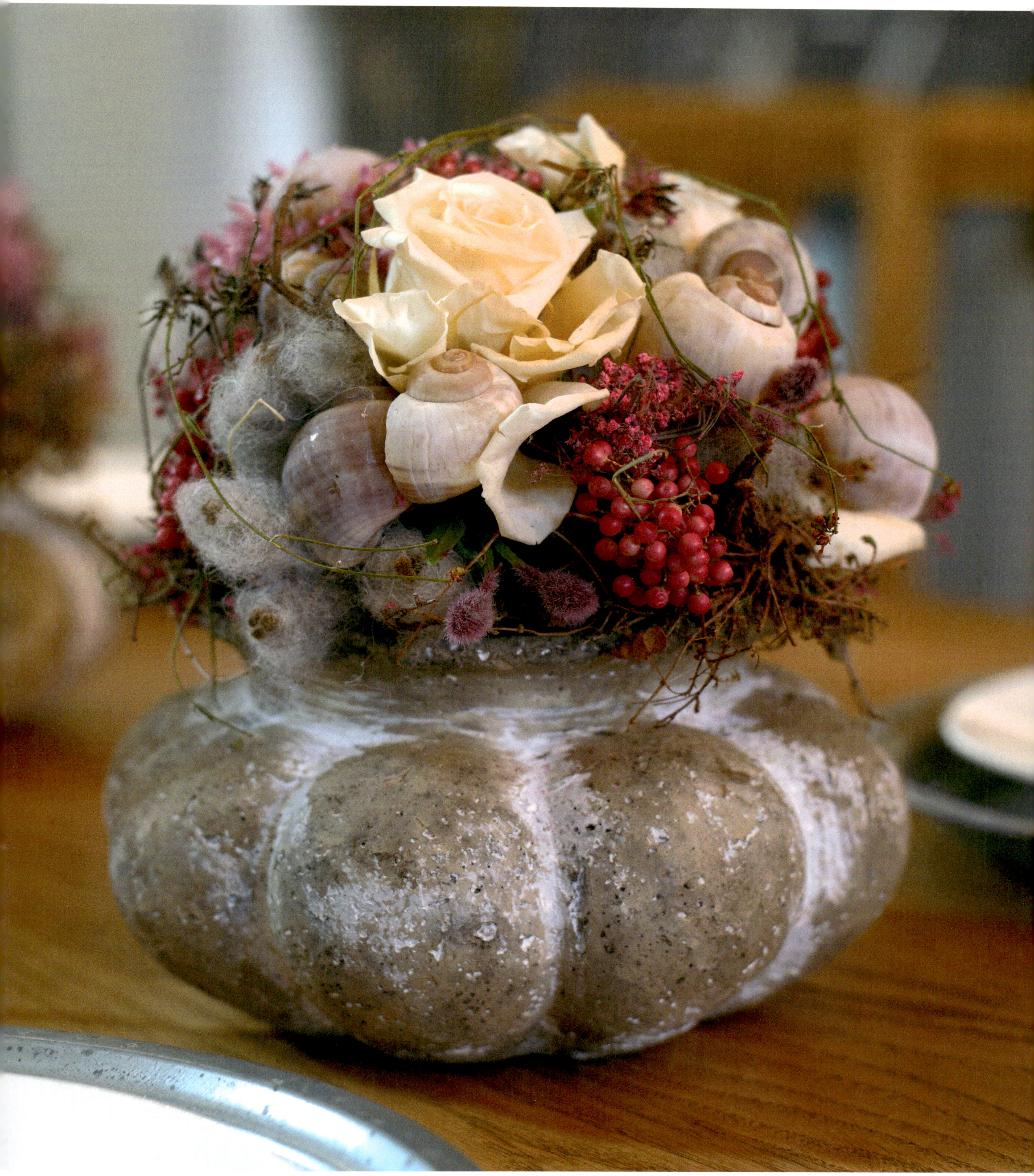

COSY BRUXELLES Tischdekoration | Table Sets

A natural piece of art decorates the table. Its basis is a rustic board, covered in fabric attached by stapling. The gnarled ivy vines attached to it each carry a floral arrangement fashioned with the aid of a floral foam ball. The votive rests in a leaf-covered straw wreath ring. The centre has been filled with floral foam to hold an arrangement.

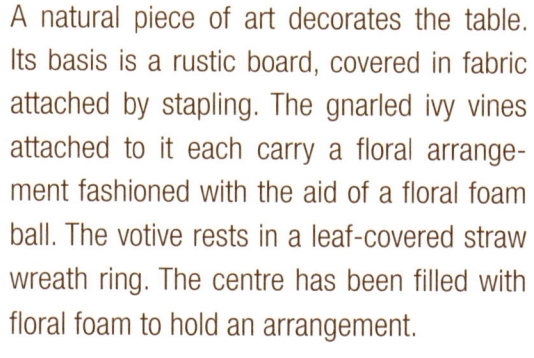

Ein Stück kunstvolle Natur ziert diesen Tisch. Basis ist ein mit Stoff betackertes rustikales Brett. Die darauf befestigten, knorrigen Efeuranken tragen je eine blumig besteckte Trockensteckschaumkugel. Das Windlicht ruht in einem mit Blättern bedeckten Strohrömer. Die mit Steckschaum ausgefüllte Kranzöffnung wird floral gestaltet.

COSY BRUXELLES Tischdekoration | Table Sets

These small table arrangements are inspired by traditional treasure chests. Small wooden boxes are filled with floral foam, flowers in bloom are either held in place by vertically inserted leaves or loosely arranged around votives. Individually or several in a row – either way a feast for the eyes, waiting to be discovered.

Diese kleinen Tischgestecke sind traditionellen Schatztruhen nachempfunden. Mal klemmen die blühenden Floralien in dem mit Steckschaum gefüllten Kistchen zwischen den senkrecht eingesteckten Blättern, mal umgeben sie locker die mittige Windlichtfüllung. Einzeln oder zu mehreren in Reihung – in jedem Fall ein Augenschmaus, den es zu entdecken gilt.

Service | Service
Unsere verwendeten Floralien, Produkte, Materialien | Floral elements, product and materials used

NEW BARCELONA

Seite 010/011 „Entree Gefäße"
Kunststoff-Gefäße, Allium, Amaranthus, Physalis, Blasenfrucht, Orchideen, Wiesengräser (künstlich), *Fallopia*, Holzfurnier, Holzstäbe, Heißkleber, Trockenblumensteckschaum

Seite 012 „Beleuchtete Raumobjekte"
Holzständer, Viburnum, Blasenfrucht, Orchideen, Orchideenwurzeln (künstlich), Monetablätter, Holzfurnier, Kugel-Tischleuchte, Holzplatte, Heißkleber

Seite 013 „Gefäßreihung"
Gefäße, Allium, Viburnum, Hortensien (künstlich), Kokosnuss, Holzscheiben, Heißkleber, Trockenblumensteckschaum

Seite 014/015 „Beklebte Halbkugeln"
Orchideen, Orchideenwurzeln (künstlich), Holzfurnier, Kork, Metallständer, Heißkleber, Styropor-Halbkugel

Seite 016 „Vorhang-Säulen"
Beeren, Blasenfrucht, Orchideen (künstlich), Holzteile, Fadenvorhang, Metallständer, Furnier, Fuß, Heißkleber, Trockenblumensteckschaum-Zylinder

Seite 017 „Kleine Fadenvorhangständer"
Allium, Viburnum, Hortensie (künstlich), Band, Furnier, Fadenreste vom Vorhang, Metallständer, Heißkleber, Trockenblumensteckschaum-Zylinder

Seite 018 „Tanzende Gefäße"
Gefäße, Orchideenblüten (künstlich), Schoten, Holzfurnier, Band, Stützdraht, Heißkleber, Trockenblumensteckschaum

Seite 019 „Grüne Gestecke"
Gefäße rechteckig, Physalis, Hortensien, Orchideen (künstlich), Gräser, Schoten, Holzscheiben, Furnierstreifen, Trockenblumensteckschaum

Seite 020/021 „Orchideen auf Holzgestell"
Gefäß, Physalis, Orchideen (künstlich), Schoten, Holzgestell, Sand

Seite 022 „Vasengruppe"
Physalis, Orchideen (künstlich), Trockenfloralien, Tapete, Holzbrett, doppelseitiges Klebeband, Farbe, Trockenblumensteckschaum

Seite 023 „Klein in groß"
Gefäße, Orchideen (künstlich), Trockenfloralien, Band, Holzfurnier, Heißkleber, Pappring, Trockenblumensteckschaum

Seite 024 „Säulentrio auf Steinen"
Orchideen (künstlich), Trockenfloralien, Steine mit Pin, Tapete, Heißkleber, Trockenblumensteckschaum

Seite 025 „Gräsersäule für Orchideen"
Gefäß, Orchideen (künstlich), Gräser, Holzfurnier, Heißkleber

Seite 026 oben „Rundliche Gefäße"
Schalen, Beeren, Orchideen (künstlich), Trockenblumensteckschaum

Seite 026 unten „Grastopf in eckigem Glas"
Grastopf (künstlich), Allium, Orchideen (künstlich), Holzfurnier, Kork

Seite 027 „Flaschenbündel"
Flaschen, Physalis, Orchideen (künstlich), Trockenmaterialien, Teichfolienband mit Steinen, Heißkleber

Seite 028 „Grüne Zylindergefäße"
Gefäße, Allium (künstlich), Trockenfloralien, Rebenbindedraht, Trockenblumensteckschaum

Seite 029 „Flaschen versponnen"
Flaschen, Orchideen (künstlich), Trockenfloralien, Kordel, Regalelemente, Heißkleber

Seite 030/031 „Objekt für die Bar"
Holzform, Physalis, Beeren, Blasenfrucht (künstlich), Monetablätter, Reedstäbe

Seite 032 „Holzskulpturen"
Gebleichte Holzform, Orchidee (künstlich), Metallständer

Seite 033 „Kleine Holzskulptur"
Holzknorren, Orchidee (künstlich), Metallständer, Heißkleber

Seite 034 „Objekt mit Kokosnussteilen"
Schale, Allium, Physalis, Orchideen (künstlich), Kokosnussteile, Bambusstäbe

Seite 035 „Raumteiler"
Bambus-Paravent, Amaranthus, Blasenfrucht, Hortensie, Orchideen, Orchideenwurzeln (künstlich), Heißkleber

Seite 036/037 „Schiefe Säule"
Allium, Physalis, Gerbera, Ranken (künstlich), Schoten, Palmfruchtzweig, Heißkleber, Metallständer

Seite 038 oben rechts „Gefäß mit Blättern"
Gefäß, Orchidee (künstlich), *Skabiosa*, Trockenblätter, Trockenblumensteckschaum

Seite 038 oben links „Gefäß mit Bündel"
Gefäß, Orchidee (künstlich), Gras, Holzfurnier, Trockenblumensteckschaum

Seite 039 „Gefäße mit Dattelfruchtstand"
Gefäße, Orchidee (künstlich), Trockenfloralien, z. B. Dattelfruchtstände, Strelitzienblätter, *Miscanthus*, Trockenblumensteckschaum

Seite 040 „Grastopf"
Grastopf (künstlich), Orchideen (künstlich), Holzfurnier, Kork, Band, Steinband, Heißkleber

Seite 041 links „Vasen-Trio"
Vasen, Orchideen (künstlich), Holzscheiben, Reedstäbe, Sand, Heißkleber

Seite 041 rechts „Wanddekoration"
Platte, Blasenfruchtranke, Hortensie (künstlich), Schoten, Heißkleber

NEW BARCELONA
Page 010/011
Lobby Vases, plastic containers, alliums, amaranthus, physalis, alyssum, orchids, meadow grass (artificial), *Fallopia*, wood veneer, wooden sticks, hot glue, dry floral foam

Page 012 "Backlit Objects"
Wooden stand, viburnum, alyssum, orchids, orchid roots (artificial), moneta leaves, wood veneer, ball table lamp, wooden board, hot glue

Page 013 "Row of Containers"
Containers, alliums, viburnum, hydrangeas (artificial), ccoconut, log slices, hot glue, dry floral foam

Page 014/015 "Decorated Half-Spheres"
Orchids, orchid roots (artificial), wood veneer, cork, metal stand, hot glue, styrofoam half-sphere

Page 016 "Curtain Pillars"
Berries, alyssum, orchids (artificial), pieces of wood, string curtain, metal stand, veneer, foot, hot glue, dry floral foam cylinder

Page 017 "Small Standing Curtains"
Alliums, viburnum, hydrangea (artificial), ribbon, veneer, string left over from curtain, metal stand, hot glue, dry floral foam cylinder

Page 018 "Dancing Jars"
Containers, orchids (artificial), pods, wood veneer, ribbon, florist wire, hot glue, dry floral foam

Page 019 "Green Arrangements"
Oblong containers, physalis, hydrangea, orchids (artificial), grasses, pods, log slices, strips of veneer, dry floral foam

Page 020/021 "Orchids on Wooden Structure"
Container, physalis, orchids (artificial), pods, wooden base structure, sand

Page 022 "Grouped Vases"
Physalis, orchids (artificial), dried floral elements, wallpaper, wooden board, double-sided adhesive tape, paint, dry floral foam

Page 023 "Small in Large"
Containers, orchids (artificial), dried floral elements, ribbon, wood veneer, hot glue, cardboard ring, dry floral foam

Page 024 "Pillar Trio on Stones"
Orchids (artificial), dried floral elements, stones with metal spike, wallpaper, hot glue, dry floral foam

Page 025 "Grass Pillar for Orchids"
Container, orchids (artificial), grasses, wood veneer, hot glue

Page 026 top "Ball Jars"
Bowls, berries, orchids (artificial), dry floral foam

Page 026 bottom "Grass Pot in Square Glass"
Grass pot (artificial), alliums, orchids (artificial), wood veneer, cork

Page 027 "Bottle Bundle"
Bottles, physalis, orchids (artificial), dried materials, pebble edging pond liner, hot glue

Page 028 "Green Cylindrical Containers"
Containers, alliums (artificial), dried floral elements, grape vine wire, dry floral foam

Page 029 "Strung Bottles"
Bottles, orchids (artificial), dried floral elements, cord, shelving elements, hot glue

Page 030/031 "Counter-Top Objects for Bar"
wooden shape, physalis, berries, alyssum (artificial), moneta leaves, giunco sticks

Page 032 "Wooden Sculptures"
Bleached wooden shape, orchid (artificial), metal stand

Page 033 "Small Wooden Sculpture"
Gnarled piece of wood, orchid (artificial), metal stand, hot glue

Page 034 "Object with Coconut Pieces"
Tray, alliums, physalis, orchids (artificial), coconut pieces, bamboo sticks

Page 035 "Room Divider"
Bamboo screen, amaranthus, alyssum, hydrangea, orchids, orchid roots (artificial), hot glue

Page 036/037 "Leaning Pillar"
Alliums, physalis, gerbera, vines (artificial), pods, palm fruit branch, hot glue, metal stand

Page 038 top right "Container with Leaves"
Container, orchid (artificial), *Scabiosa*, dried leaves, dry floral foam

Page 038 top left "Container with Bunch"
Container, orchid (artificial), grass, wood veneer, dry floral foam

Page 039 "Containers with Date Seed Heads"
Containers, orchid (artificial), dried floral elements, e.g. date seed heads, bird-of-paradise leaves, *Miscanthus*, dry floral foam

Page 040 "Grass Pot"
Grass pot (artificial), orchids (artificial), wood veneer, cork, ribbon, pebble ribbon, hot glue

Page 041 left "Vases Trio"
Vases, orchids (artificial), log slices, giunco sticks, sand, hot glue

Page 041 right "Wall Decoration"
Board, alyssum vine, hydrangea (artificial), pods, hot glue

FRESH AMSTERDAM

Seite 044/045
„Stiefmütterchen im Seidenpapier"
Vasen, Stiefmütterchen (künstlich), Wilde Möhre, Sprühfarbe, Seidenpapier, Wachs, Steckdraht, Trockenblumensteckschaum

Seite 046 „Gefüllte Papierrollen"
Glasgefäße, Stiefmütterchen, Vergissmeinnicht (künstlich), Pappe, Sprühfarbe, Farbe, Heißkleber, Pinholder, Klebeband, Trockenblumensteckschaum-Stange

Seite 047 links unten „Moosschale"
Keramikschale, Vergissmeinnicht (künstlich), Moos, Haften, Zierdraht, Trockenblumensteckschaum

Seite 047 rechts unten „Strauß mit Filzschnüren"
Glasschale, Disteln, Stiefmütterchen, Vergissmeinnicht (künstlich), Wolle, Heißkleber

Seite 048 „Blaues Vasen-Trio"
Keramikvasen, Mohnkapseln (künstlich), *Craspedia*, Wilde Möhre, Sprühlack, Trockenblumensteckschaum

Seite 049 „Vasenfüllung mit Wachs"
Keramikvasen, Stiefmütterchen (künstlich), *Craspedia*, Wachs, Farbe, Trockenblumensteckschaum

Seite 050/051 „Raumobjekt mit Wolle"
Mohn (künstlich), *Craspedia*, Blätter, Wachs, Wolle, Zierdraht, Blitzbeton, Eisenstange, Trockenblumensteckschaum-Stange

Seite 052/053 „Wanddekoration mit Blütentaschen"
Mohn, Vergissmeinnicht (künstlich), *Miscanthus*, Trockenfloralien, Wolle, Wachs, Filz, Spanplatte, Farbe, Drahtgitter, Heißkleber

Seite 054/055 „Kranz in Styroporplatte"
Brett, Ranunkel, Stiefmütterchen, Vergissmeinnicht (künstlich), Skabiosen, Disteln, Reedstäbe, Wachs, Filz, Farbe, Styropor, Heißkleber

Seite 056 „Gefüllte blaue Gläser"
Glasgefäße, Mohn (künstlich), Mohnkapseln, Peddigrohr, Sprühfarbe, Sand, Trockenblumensteckschaum

Seite 057 „Vergissmeinnichtstrauß"
Glasgefäß, Vergissmeinnicht (künstlich), Wachs, Wolle, Seidenpapier

FRESH AMSTERDAM

Page 044/045 "Pansies in Silk Paper"
Vases, pansies (artificial), wild carrot, spray paint, silk paper, wax, fixing wire, dry floral foam

Page 046 "Filled paper tubes"
Glass jars, pansies, forget-me-nots (artificial), cardboard, spray paint, paint, hot glue, pin holder, adhesive tape, dry floral foam bar

Page 047 bottom left "Moss bowl"
Ceramic bowl, forget-me-nots (artificial), moss, mossing pins, decorative wire, dry floral foam

Page 047 bottom right "Bouquet with Felt String"
Glass bowl, thistles, pansies, forget-me-nots (artificial), wool, hot glue

Page 048 "Trio of Blue Vases"
Ceramic vases, poppy pods (artificial), *Craspedia*, wild carrot, spray paint, dry floral foam

Page 049 "Wax Filled Vase"
Ceramic vases, pansies (artificial), *Craspedia*, wax, paint, dry floral foam

Page 050/051 "Decorative Object with Wool"
Poppies (artificial), *Craspedia*, leaves, wax, wool, decorative wire, fast set concrete, iron rod, dry floral foam bar

Page 052/053 "Wall Arrangement with Flower Filled Bags"
Poppies, forget-me-nots (artificial), *Miscanthus*, dried floral elements, wool, wax, felt, chipboard batten, paint, wire mesh, hot glue

Page 054/055 "Wreath on Styrofoam Board"
Board, ranunculi, pansies, forget-me-nots (artificial), scabiosas, thistles, giunco sticks, wax, felt, paint, styrofoam, hot glue

Page 056 "Filled Blue Jars"
Glass jars, poppies (artificial), poppy pods, rattan cane, spray paint, sand, dry floral foam

Page 057 "Forget-me-not Bouquet"
Glass jar, forget-me-nots (artificial), wax, wool, silk paper, paint, styrofoam, hot glue

YOUNG BRITISH

Seite 060/061 „XXL-Vasen"
Vasen, Orchideen, Beerenzweige (künstlich), Magnolienblätter, Flechtenzweige, *Physalis*, Kirschzweige, Wickeldraht, Papierband, Trockenblumensteckschaum

Seite 062 „Perlmuttgefäß mit Lila-Purpur-Schmuck"
Perlmuttgefäß, Allium, Beerenzweige, Mohn (künstlich), Flechtenzweige, Kirschzweige, Trockenblumensteckschaum

Seite 063 „Magnolienbäumchen"
Gefäß, Beerenzweige (künstlich), Flechtenzweige, Kirschzweige, Magnolienzweige, Trockenblumensteckschaum

Seite 064/065 „Rankenbogen"
Silberpokal, Beeren, Mohn (künstlich), *Lonicera henryi*, Magnolienblätter, Zierdraht, Granulat, Metallstange, Heißkleber, Trockenblumensteckschaum

Seite 066 „Muschelbogen"
Tillandsia usneoides, Hortensien, Magnolienblätter, Heu, Muscheln, Peddigrohr, Wickeldraht, Zierdraht, Heißkleber, Seil

Seite 067 „Tillandsien-Hörner"
Kerzenleuchter, verschiedene textile Blüten, *Tillandsia usneoides*, Heu, Zierdraht, Wickeldraht, Heißkleber

Seite 068 oben „Kugel mit Federn"
Metallfuß, Allium, Ranunkeln, Rosen (künstlich), Zierdraht, Heißkleber, Trockenblumensteckschaum-Kugel

Seite 068 unten „Gläser für die Bar"
Glasgefäße, Allium, Ranunkeln, Rosen (künstlich), Leder, Kerzen, Zierdraht, Trockenblumensteckschaum

Seite 069 „Ledergefäß"
Silbergefäß, Mohnblüten (künstlich), Phormiumblätter, Leder, Pappe, Schneewatte als Polster, Zierstecknadeln, Tackernadeln, Heißkleber, Trockenblumensteckschaum

Seite 070/071 „Federkugel"
Kerzenleuchter, Beeren, Orchideen, Pfingstrosen, Ranken (künstlich), Trockenfloralien, Federn, Zierdraht, Heißkleber, Styropor-Halbkugel, Trockenblumensteckschaum

Seite 072/073 „Schlanke Füllhörner"
Allium, Beeren, Hortensien, Pfingstrosen, Ranunkeln (künstlich), Magnolienblätter, Silberpappelblätter, Peddigrohr, Heu, Band, Zierdraht, Floralkleber, Metallstange mit Fuß, Heißkleber

Seite 074 „Kranz"
Beeren, Hortensien, Orchidee (künstlich), *Tillandsia usneoides*, Flechtenzweige, Muscheln, Kerzen, Gläser, Kappaplatte, Stoff, Kerzenleuchterfüße, Heißkleber, Trockenblumensteckschaum-Kranz

Seite 074 unten „Blütentorte"
Silperschale, Allium, Pfingstrosen, Rosen, Statice (künstlich), Magnolienblätter, Proteen, Band, Stecknadeln, Trockenblumensteckschaum-Zylinder

Seite 075 „Kranz mit Capiz-Muscheln"
Beeren, Ranken, Rosen (künstlich), *Tillandsia usneoides*, Trockenfrüchte, Muscheln, Band, Heißkleber, Strohrömer

Seite 076/077 „Pokal mit Schneckenhäusern"
Gefäß, Iris (künstlich), *Tillandsia usneoides*, Kirschzweig, Schneckenhäuser, Tonkinstäbe, Sprühfarbe, Heißkleber, Trockenblumensteckschaum

Seite 078 „Wellness-Schale"
Schale, Allium, Iris (künstlich), Kelp Strips, *Tillandsia usneoides*, Muscheln, Stoff, Trockenblumensteckschaum

Seite 079 „Iris-Pokale"
Iris (künstlich), Flechte, Zierdraht, Ständer, Blei, Heißkleber, Trockenblumensteckschaum-Kugel

Seite 080 „Raumschmuck für Relaxraum"
Gefäß, Allium, Iris, Orchideen (künstlich), Gräser, Muscheln, Stoff, Heißkleber, Trockenblumensteckschaum

Seite 081 „Zusammengesetzte Blüte"
Leucophyta, Astrantia, Iris, Beeren (künstlich), *Tillandsia usneoides*, Flechte, Muscheln, Blei, Heißkleber, Zierdraht, Steckdraht

YOUNG BRITISH

Page 060/061 "XXL Vases"
Vases, orchids, twigs with berries (artificial), magnolia leaves, lichen twigs, *Physalis*, cherry tree twigs, binding wire, paper ribbon, dry floral foam

Page 062 "Mother-of-Pearl Container with Purple-Crimson Arrangement"
Mother-of-pearl jar, alliums, twigs with berries, poppies (artificial), lichen twigs, cherry tree twigs, dry floral foam

Page 063 "Small Magnolia Trees"
Container, twigs with berries (artificial), lichen twigs, cherry tree twigs, magnolia twigs, dry floral foam

Page 064/065 "Arch"
Silver goblet, berries, poppies (artificial), *Lonicera henryi*, magnolia leaves, decorative wire, granules, metal rod, hot glue, dry floral foam

Page 066 "Seashell Arch"
Tillandsia usneoides, hydrangea, magnolia leaves, hay, shells, rattan cane, binding wire, decorative wire, hot glue, rope

Page 067 "Tillandsia Horns"
Candle stick, assorted fabric flowers, *Tillandsia usneoides*, hay, decorative wire, binding wire, hot glue

Page 068 top "Ball with Feathers"
Metal stand, alliums, ranunculi, roses (artificial), decorative wire, hot glue, dry floral foam ball

Page 068 bottom "Counter-Top Glasses for the Bar"
Glass jars, alliums, ranunculi, roses (artificial), leather, candles, decorative wire, dry floral foam

Page 069 "Leather Container"
Silver jar, poppies (artificial), phormium fronds, leather, cardboard, cushion of cotton batting snow, decorative pins, staples, hot glue, dry floral foam

Page 070/071 "Feather Ball"
Candle stick, berries, orchids, peonies, vines (artificial), dried floral elements, feathers, decorative wire, hot glue, styrofoam half-sphere, dry floral foam

Page 072/073 "Tall Cornucopias"
Alliums, berries, hydrangeas, peonies, ranunculi (artificial), magnolia leaves, white poplar leaves, rattan cane, hay ribbon, decorative wire, floral adhesive, metal rod on stand, hot glue

Page 074 "Wreath"
Berries, hydrangeas, orchid (artificial), *Tillandsia usneoides*, lichen twigs, shells,

candles, glasses, kapa board, fabric, candle stick feet, hot glue, dry floral foam ring

Page 074 bottom "Flower Cake"
Silver bowl, alliums, peonies, roses, limonium (artificial), magnolia leaves, proteas, ribbon, pins, dry floral foam cylinder

Page 075 "Wreath with Capiz Shells"
Berries, vines, roses (artificial), *Tillandsia usneoides*, dried fruit, shells, ribbon, hot glue, straw wreath ring

Page 076/077 "Goblet with Snail Shells"
Container, iris (artificial), *Tillandsia usneoides*, cherry tree twig, snail shells, tonkin cane sticks, spray paint, hot glue, dry floral foam

Page 078 "Spa Bowl"
Bowl, alliums, iris (artificial), kelp strips, *Tillandsia usneoides,* shells, fabric, dry floral foam

Page 079 "Iris Goblets"
Iris (artificial), lichen, decorative wire, stand, lead, hot glue, dry floral foam ball

Page 080 "Arrangement for Relaxation Room"
Container, alliums, iris, orchids (artificial), grasses, shells, fabric, hot glue, dry floral foam

Page 081 "Flower Composition"
Leucophyta, astrantia, iris, berries (artificial), *Tillandsia usneoides*, lichen, shells, lead, hot glue, decorative wire, fixing wire

LIGHT COPENHAGEN

Seite 084/085 „Entreedekoration in Würfelform"
Schiefergefäß, Ammi, Physalis, Bärlauch, Wiesenkräuter (künstlich), Birkenrinde, Birkengrundgerüst, Reedstäbe, Quarzsand

Seite 086 „Pflanzenbank in Rot"
Bodengefäß, Allium, Agapanthus, Bärlauch, Knoblauch, Wiesenkräuter (künstlich), Aluminiumdraht, Metallgase, Fliegendrahtgitter, Trockenblumensteckschaum

Seite 087 „Glaswürfel-Quartett"
Glaskuben, Allium, Ammi, Asclepias, Physalis, Wiesenkräuter (künstlich), Birkenrinde, Band, Trockenblumensteckschaum

Seite 088 „Glaskuben-Reihung"
Glaskuben, Ammi, Physalis, Bärlauch, Wiesenkräuter (künstlich), Birkenrinde, Reedstäbe, Quarzsand, Trockenblumensteckschaum

Seite 089 „Birkenaststelen in Würfeln"
Betonwürfelgefäße, Allium, Bärlauch, Wiesenkräuter (künstlich), Birkenzweige, Kieselsteine, Trockenblumensteckschaum

Seite 090 „Glaswannen-Collage"
Glasgefäße, Allium, Bärlauch, Knoblauch, Wiesenkräuter (künstlich), Strelitzienblätter, Birkenrindenstreifen, Stahlseil

Seite 092 „Blumige Betonplatte"
Asclepias, Wisteria, Physalis (künstlich), Stahlseil, Spanndraht, Beton, Tischläufer

Seite 093 „Sideboard-Objekt"
Ammi, Asclepias, Wiesenkräuter (künstlich), Reedstäbe, Drahtgitter, Standfuß aus Metall, Aluminiumrohr, Schieferplatte

Seite 094 „Reedstäbe-Reihung"
Betonkubus, Asclepias, Physalis, Wiesengräser (künstlich), Reedstäbe, Trockenblumensteckschaum

Seite 095 „Glaswannen-Gesteck"
Glaswürfel, Agapanthus, Asclepias, Wiesengräser (künstlich), Birkenrindenstreifen, Reedstäbe, Quarzsand, Trockenblumensteckschaum

Seite 096 „Blüten-Schichtung"
Schiefergefäß, Ammi, Bärlauch, Wiesenkräuter (künstlich), Birkenrinde, Filzstreifen, Heißkleber

Seite 097 „Blüten-Steckgefäß"
Betonkubus, Allium, Ammi, Physalis, Wiesengräser (künstlich), Reedstäbe, Gips, Trockenblumensteckschaum

Seite 098 „Glaswürfelschmuck"
Glaskubus, Agapanthus, Ammi, Knoblauch, Bärlauch, Wiesengräser (künstlich), Gräser, Birkenrindenstreifen, Kieselsteine, Drahtgaze, Hasendraht

Seite 099 „Birkenzweige in Betonzylindern"
Betongefäße, Asclepias, Festuca, Miscanthus (künstlich), Birkenzweige, Birkenrinde, Trockenblumensteckschaum

Seite 100 „Raumgefäß mit Drahtgazemanschette"
Betongefäß, Agapanthus, Ammi, Bärlauch, Knoblauch, Wiesenkräuter (künstlich), Gräser, Birkenrindenstreifen, Maschendraht, Drahtgaze, Spanndraht, Trockenblumensteckschaum

LIGHT COPENHAGEN

Page 084/085 "Foyer Arrangement in Cubes"
Slate tray, ammi, physalis, wild garlic, meadow herbs (artificial), birch bark, basic birch structure, giunco sticks, silica sand

Page 086 "Plant Box in Red"
Floor vase, alliums, agapanthus, wild garlic, garlic, meadow herbs (artificial), aluminium wire, metal gauze, flywire screening mesh, dry floral foam

Page 087 "Glass Cube Quartet"
Glass cubes, ammi, asclepia, physalis, wild garlic, meadow herbs (artificial), birch bark, ribbon, dry floral foam

Page 088 "Row of Glass Cubes"
Glass cubes, ammi, physalis, wild garlic, meadow herbs (artificial), birch bark, giunco sticks, silica sand, dry floral foam

Page 089 "Birch Branches in Cubes"
Cubic concrete containers, alliums, wild garlic, meadow herbs (artificial), birch branches, pebbles, dry floral foam

Page 090 "Glass Trough Collage"
Glass troughs, alliums, wild garlic, garlic, meadow herbs (artificial), bird-of-paradise leaves, birch bark strips, steel rope

Page 092 "Floral Concrete Slab"
Asclepia, wisteria, physalis (artificial), steel rope, guy wire, concrete, table runner

Page 093 "Woven Sideboard Arrangement"
Ammi, asclepia, meadow herbs (artificial), giunco sticks, wire mesh, metal stand, aluminium tube, slate plate

Page 094 "Giunco Stick Row"
Concrete cube, asclepia, physalis, meadow grasses (artificial), giunco sticks, dry floral foam

Page 095 "Glass Cube Arrangement"
Glass cubes, agapanthus, asclepia, meadow grasses (artificial), birch bark strips, giunco sticks, silica sand, dry floral foam

Page 096 "Tray with Floral Potpourri"
Slate tray, alliums, wild garlic, meadow herbs (artificial), birch bark, felt strips, hot glue

Page 097 "Container with Flower Arrangement"
Concrete container, alliums, ammi, physalis, meadow grasses (artificial), giunco sticks, gypsum plaster, dry floral foam

Page 098 "Arrangement in Glass Cube"
Glass cube, agapanthus, ammi, wild garlic, garlic, meadow grasses (artificial), grasses, birch bark strips, pebbles, wire gauze, chicken wire

Page 099 "Birch Twigs in Concrete Cylinders"
Concrete containers, asclepia, festuce, miscanthus (artificial), birch branches, birch bark, dry floral foam

Page 100 "Floor Vase with Wire Gauze Collar"
Concrete container, agapanthus, ammi, wild garlic, garlic, meadow herbs (artificial), grasses, birch bark strips, wire netting, wire gauze, guy wire, dry floral foam

COSY BRUXELLES

Seite 104 „Entree-Stabgesteck"
Gefäße, Hortensien, Edelweiß, Rosen (künstlich), Tillandsia usneoides, Canella, Pfefferbeeren, Bänder, Steckdraht, Zierdraht, Heißkleber, Stahlstange, Floralkleber, Trockenblumensteckschaum-Zylinder

Seite 105 „Blume im Wollkragen"
Gefäße, Physalis, Ranunkeln, Rosen, Thymian (künstlich), Skabiose, Filzschnur

Seite 106 „Dekorierter Hängering"
Allium, Physalis, Rosen (künstlich), Schleierkraut, Wollziest, Wiesen- und Gartenkräuter, Heu, Sisal, Jute, Wolle, Packband, Zierdraht, Zeitungspapier, Weidenring, Metallring, Drahtseil

Seite 107 „Thekendekoration mit Rosenkugeln"
Gefäß, Rosen (künstlich), Eichenblätter, Canella, Schleierkraut, Tillandsia usneoides, Moos, Efeuranken, Heißkleber, Trockenblumensteckschaum-Kugel

Seite 108 „Kränze auf Holzstumpf"
Allium, Lunaria, Beeren, Ranken (künstlich), Skabiosen, Schleierkraut, Canella, Wolle, Jute, Kokosfaser, Band, Zierdraht, Steckdraht, Metallstifte, Strohrömer, Holzstumpf

Seite 109 „Wandzopf"
Allium, Beeren, Ranunkeln (künstlich), Schleierkraut, Heu, Sisal, Steckdraht, Zierdraht, Flauschwolle, Band

Seite 110 „Heugestecke auf Holzstumpf"
Allium, Rosen (künstlich), Skabiosen, Schleierkraut, Beeren, Wiesengräser, Heu, Zierdraht, Heißkleber, Holzstumpf, Trockenblumensteckschaum

Seite 111 „Kleiner Heukokon"
Edelweiß (künstlich), Lunaria annua, Stachys, Päonienblüten, Heu, Schneckenhäuser, Wolle, Holzstumpf, Trockenblumensteckschaum

Seite 112 „Wandbilder"
Tablett, Allium, Ranunkeln (künstlich), Stachys, Teebusch, Schneckenhäuser, Spitzenband, Zierdraht, Heißkleber

Seite 113 „Ausgefüllter Wandkranz"
Physalis, Ranunkel (künstlich), Skabiosen, Band, Kranz, Pappe, Heißkleber, Floralkleber, Trockenblumensteckschaum

Seite 114 „Große Tresendekoration"
Gefäß, Seidenblumen, Allium (künstlich), verschiedene Trockenfloralien, Waldfarn, Sisalstrick, Tonkinstäbe, Heißkleber, Trockenblumensteckschaum

Seite 114 unten „Gehäkelter Kranz"
Physalis, Rosen (künstlich), Tillandsia usneoides, Skabiose, Canella, Schleierkraut, Wolle, Band, Steckdraht, Zierdraht, Pappe, Heißkleber, Floralkleber

Seite 115 „Heugestecke mit Füßen"
Physalis, Edelweiß, Rosen (künstlich), Stachys, Schleierkraut, Canella, Heu, Zweige, Schneckenhäuser, Band, Stoff, Spitze, Splittstäbe, Zierdraht, Haften, Heißkleber, Trockenblumensteckschaum

Seite 116 „Thekenetagere"
Etagere, Flaschen, Gläser, Allium, Edelweiß, Ranunkeln, Rosen (künstlich), Schleierkraut, Statice, Heu, Wolle, Spitzenband, Blechherz, Zierdraht, Geschirrtücher, Trockenblumensteckschaum-Kugel

Seite 117 oben links „Craquelee-Vasenfüllung"
Vase, Edelweiß, Rose (künstlich), *Tillandsia usneoides*, Canella, Geschirrtuch

Seite 117 oben rechts „Korbgefäß mit Strickrand"
Korb, Edelweiß (künstlich), Heu, Wolle, Herzaccessoire, Zierdraht, Schmucknadeln

Seite 118/119 „Spitzen-Tischgestecke"
Rose (künstlich), *Lunaria annua*, Schleierkraut, Skabiose, Canella, Stoff, Spitzenband, Schneckenhäuser, Trockenblumensteckschaum-Zylinder

Seite 120 „Tischschmuck-Reihung"
Gefäße, Edelweiß, Rosen (künstlich), Canella, Geschirrtücher, Holzstamm, Zierdraht, Heißkleber, Nagel, Trockenblumensteckschaum

Seite 121 „Gestecke mit Schneckenhäusern"
Gefäß, Canella, Gräser, Rosen (künstlich), Schneckenhäuser, Filzwolle, Heißkleber, Trockenblumensteckschaum

Seite 122 „Tischdekoration mit Ast"
Holzbrett, Rosen (künstlich), *Tillandsia usneoides*, Canella, Schleierkraut, Skabiose, Eichenblätter, Nägel, Stoff, Heißkleber, Tackernadeln, Trockenblumensteckschaum-Kugel

Seite 123 „Windlicht im Kranz"
Glas, Rosen, Beeren (künstlich), Apfelblatt, Thymian, Gräser, Heu, Steckdraht, Stecknadeln, Strohrömer, Kerze, Heißkleber, Trockenblumensteckschaum

Seite 124 „Kleine Blumen-Schatzkiste"
Gefäß, Allium, Hortensien, Rosen (künstlich), *Tillandsia usneoides*, Schleierkraut, Apfelblätter, Heu, Band, Jute, Heißkleber, Trockenblumensteckschaum

Seite 125 „Leuchtende Blumenkiste"
Gefäß, Allium, Beeren, Hortensien (künstlich), Schleierkraut, Apfelblätter, Thymian, Gläser, Kerzen, Trockenblumensteckschaum

COSY BRUXELLES

Page 104 "Arrangement on Rods in Foyer"
Containers, hydrangeas, edelweiss, roses (artificial), *Tillandsia usneoides*, canella, pepper berries, ribbons, fixing wire, decorative wire, hot glue, steel rod, gloral adhesive, dry floral foam cylinder

Page 105 "Flowers in Wool Collar"
Containers, physalis, ranunculi, roses, thyme (artificial), scabiosa, felt string

Page 106 "Hanging Arrangement"
Alliums, physalis, roses (artificial), *Gypsophila*, *Stachys byzantina*, meadow and garden herbs, hay, sisal, jute, wool, packing tape, decorative wire, newspaper, willow ring, metal ring, piano wire

Page 107 "Counter Arrangement with Rose Balls"
Container, roses (artificial), oak leaves, canella, *Gypsophila*, *Tillandsia usneoides*, moss, ivy vines, hot glue, dry floral foam ball

Page 108 "Wreaths on Logs"
Alliums, lunaria, berries, vines (artificial), *Scabiosa*, *Gypsophila*, canella, wool, jute, coir, ribbon, decorative wire, fixing wire, metal pins, straw wreath ring, logs

Page 109 "Braided Hanging Arrangement"
Alliums, berries, ranunculi (artificial), *Gypsophila*, hay, sisal, fixing wire, decorative wire, fluffy wool, Ribbon

Page 110 "Hay Arrangements on Logs"
Alliums, roses (artificial), *Scabiosa*, *Gypsophila*, berries, meadow grasses, hay, decorative wire, hot glue, logs, dry floral foam

Page 111 "Small Hay Cocoon"
Edelweiss (artificial), *Lunaria annua*, *Stachys*, peonies, hay, snail shells, wool, log, dry floral foam

Page 112 "Wall Decorations"
Tray, alliums, ranunculi (artificial), *Stachys*, tea bush, snail shells, lace ribbon, decorative wire, hot glue

Page 113 "Filled Wall Wreath"
Physalis, ranunculi (artificial), *Scabiosa*, ribbon, wreath, cardboard, hot glue, floral adhesive, dry floral foam

Page 114 "Large Counter Arrangement"
Container, silk flowers, alliums (artificial), assorted dried floral elements, lady fern, sisal rope, tonkin cane sticks, hot glue, dry floral foam

Page 114 bottom "Crochet Wreath"
Physalis, roses (artificial), *Tillandsia usneoides*, *Scabiosa*, canella, *Gypsophila*, wool, ribbon, fixing wire, decorative wire, cardboard, hot glue, floral adhesive

Page 115 "Hay Arrangements with Feet"
Physalis, edelweiss, roses (artificial), *Stachys*, *Gypsophila*, canella, hay, twigs, snail shells, ribbon, fabric, lace, split canes, decorative wire, mossing pins, hot glue, dry floral foam

Page 116 "Counter Cake Stand"
Cake stand, bottles, glasses, alliums, edelweiss, ranunculi, roses (artificial), *Gypsophila*, *Limonium*, hay, wool, lace ribbon, tin heart, decorative wire, tea towels, dry floral foam ball

Page 117 top left "Filled Crackle Glaze Vase"
Vase, edelweiss, rose (artificial), *Tillandsia usneoides*, canella, tea towel

Page 117 top right "Coir Container with Knitted Collar"
Basket, edelweiss (artificial), hay, wool, decorative heart, decorative wire, decorative pins

Page 118/119 "Lacy Table Arrangements"
Roses (artificial), *Lunaria annua*, *Gypsophila*, scabiosa, canella, fabric, lace ribbon, snail shells, dry floral foam cylinder

Page 120 "Row of Table Arrangements"
Containers, edelweiss, roses (artificial), canella, tea towels, logs, decorative wire, hot glue, nail, dry floral foam

Page 121 "Snail Shell Arrangements"
Container, canella, grasses, roses (artificial), snail shells, felt wool, hot glue, dry floral foam

Page 122 "Table Arrangement with Branch"
Wooden board, roses (artificial), *Tillandsia usneoides*, canella, *Gypsophila*, *Scabiosa*, oak leaves, nails, fabric, hot glue, staples, dry floral foam ball

Page 123 "Votive in Wreath"
Glass, roses, berries (artificial), apple leaves, thyme, grasses, hay, fixing wire, pins, straw, wreath ring, candle, hot glue, dry floral foam

Page 124 "Small Floral Treasure Chest"
Container, alliums, hydrangeas, roses (artificial), *Tillandsia usneoides*, *Gypsophila*, apple leaves, hay, ribbon, jute, hot glue, dry floral foam

Page 125 "Candle-Lit Floral Box"
Container, alliums, berries, hydrangeas (artificial), *Gypsophila*, apple leaves, thyme, glasses, candles, dry floral foam

RICHTIG PRÄSENTIEREN ERFOLGREICH VERKAUFEN

Damit Sie Ihren Kunden dauerhafte Floristik in den jeweiligen Stilwelten im Geschäft präsentieren können, bieten wir die dazu passenden Stimmungsposter zum kostenlosen Download an.

WELL PRESENTED – SUCCESSFULLY SOLD
We offer matching downloadable mood posters for free to allow you to display your permanent floral arrangements in a shop environment in their respective style worlds.

www.blooms.de/dauerhaftdownload

ERFOLGREICH
mit Trockenblumen und Naturmaterialien

Als einer der führenden Anbieter von Trockenblumen und dekorativen Produkten aus Naturmaterialien bietet Auroflor den Handelspartnern qualitativ hochwertige, renditestarke und saisonal abgestimmte Produkte für zeitgemäße Floristik im Trend.

Successful with dried flowers and natural materials

As one of the leading suppliers of dried flowers and decorative elements made from natural materials, Auroflor provides its retail partners with top-quality, extremely profitable and contemporary floristry products to match all seasons.

AUROFLOR GmbH & Co KG
Natur, Floristik & Design

AUROFLOR GmbH & Co.KG

Industriestr. 28
D - 91781 Weißenburg
T +49 (0) 9141-8595-0
F +49 (0) 9141-8595-30
mail@auroflor.de
www.auroflorservice.de

AM PULS DER ZEIT
mit künstlichen Blumen und Pflanzen

Als Vollsortimenter im Bereich künstlicher Blumen und Pflanzen, als Spezialist für Kunst-Bäume bis zu einer Höhe von vier Metern und Lieferant von Dekorations- und Geschenkartikeln für Haus und Garten gehört Gasper zu den führenden Unternehmen der Branche.

Contemporary with artificial flowers and plants

As stockist of a wide range of artificial flowers and plants, specialising in artificial trees up to four metres high, gifts and decorative accessories for home and garden, Gasper is one of the industry's leading suppliers.

GASPER

GASPER GmbH
ACCESSOIRES FÜR HAUS UND GARTEN

Am Grott 4
D - 51147 Köln
T +49 (0) 2203-96669-0
F +49 (0) 2203-96669-41
gasper@gasper.de
www.gasper.de

Wir danken sehr herzlich,
dass wir in folgenden **Räumen** fotografieren durften:

Seite 008-019, 030-041, 098-101
Sheraton Hotel, Hannover, www.sheratonpelikanhannover.com

Seite 020-029
Park Inn, Bielefeld, www.park-inn-bielefeld.de

Seite 042-057
Wirbelsäulenzentrum Hannover, www.rueckenprofis.de

Seite 058-081, 102-125
Hotel & Spa Gräflicher Park, Bad Driburg, www.graeflicher-park.de

Seite 082-097
Degardo GmbH, Bad Oeynhausen, www.degardo.de

We would like to extend our thanks for being granted
permission to take photographs in the following **locations**:

Page 008-019, 030-041, 098-101
Sheraton Hotel, Hannover, www.sheratonpelikanhannover.com

Page 020-029
Park Inn, Bielefeld, www.park-inn-bielefeld.de

Page 042-057
Wirbelsäulenzentrum Hannover, www.rueckenprofis.de

Page 058-081, 102-125
Hotel & Spa Gräflicher Park, Bad Driburg, www.graeflicher-park.de

Page 082-097
Degardo GmbH, Bad Oeynhausen, www.degardo.de

DANKE THANKS

Wir danken allen Models:

Nicole Brinkmeier, Hannah Flocke, Ilka Jacobus, Hedda Janssen, Benjamin Mesch, Anna Müller, Helena Müller, Lars Rüther, Tanja Tacke, Melanie Tiemann, Cynthia Wang, Carolin Wübbels

We would like thank the models:

Nicole Brinkmeier, Hannah Flocke, Ilka Jacobus, Hedda Janssen, Benjamin Mesch, Anna Müller, Helena Müller, Lars Rüther, Tanja Tacke, Melanie Tiemann, Cynthia Wang, Carolin Wübbels

Wir danken folgenden Firmen für das Zurverfügungstellen von Produkten:

ASA, Art-Can-Del, Auroflor, Bauholz, Bel'Arte, Buco, D&M Depot, Degardo, Dekoprojekt S. Scheuerer, Florissima, Gasper, Halbach, Lehner Wolle 3, PTMD, Sandra Rich, Scheulen, Smithers-Oasis

We would like to thank the following companies for making their products available to us:

ASA, Art-Can-Del, Auroflor, Bauholz, Bel'Arte, Buco, D&M Depot, Degardo, Dekoprojekt S. Scheuerer, Florissima, Gasper, Halbach, Lehner Wolle 3, PTMD, Sandra Rich, Scheulen, Smithers-Oasis